PIONEER TRAILS,
TRIALS AND TRIUMPHS

PIONEER TRAILS, TRIALS AND TRIUMPHS

LAURA HARDIN CARSON

FOUNDATIONS *of* GRACE PUBLISHING
HARRISBURG, OHIO

Copyright © 2020 Foundations of Grace Publishing

Publisher's Foreword copyright by M. A. Robinette
Main text originally copyright 1927 by J. H. Merriam

Cover design by Joshua Narwold
Interior design by Kyle Shepherd

Published by
Foundations of Grace Publishing
P.O. Box 261
Harrisburg, Ohio 43126
www.FoundationsOfGrace.org

In cooperation with
Mission To Myanmar
www.MissionToMyanmar.com

ISBN: 978-1-7343499-8-6
Library of Congress Control Number: 2020902491

For questions or more information, email us at
FoundationsOfGracePub@gmail.com

To my dear friends
JOHN AND HELEN DRYDEN

whose strong purposeful lives have ever been an inspiration to courage and best effort; and who, standing within the inner court of my life, have at every time of crisis been ready to offer the incense of understanding, sympathy and help, so delicately tendered, during a never-failing and precious friendship extending over more than forty years, this book is affectionately dedicated.

CONTENTS

Publisher's Foreword ix
Introduction: The Apostles to the Chins 1

PART 1
Antecedents and Beginnings

1 Family, Childhood, and School Days 7
2 Conversion and Pioneer Hardships 24
3 College and Call to Mission Work 35
4 First Voyage to Burma 48
5 Early Experiences as a Missionary 56
6 Vacation Days and Missionary Trials 66
7 Shwe Po and Aung Bwin 72
8 Marriage and First Mission to Chins 79
9 First Return to America 88
10 Ma Wine and Ma Pu 93
11 Jungle Trips 98
12 Ko So, Ko Min, and Maung Tun 104
13 Queer Customs and Thrilling Experiences 108
14 Second Return to America 114

PART 2
Founding the Haka Mission

15 Beyond the Pale of Civilization 121
16 Loving the Unlovely 135
17 Working Under Difficulties 138
18 Emergency Return to America 144

19	A Medical Missionary for Haka	148
20	Tang Tsin and Tsong Hkam	152
21	Mr. Carson's Last Tour	157
22	Carrying On Alone	166
23	A Leper's Fate and the Sequel	171
24	New Recruits and Third Return	175
25	Back to the Field Again	179
26	Meeting New Problems	184
27	Native Insurrection—During World War	187
28	Dealing with Famine and "Flu"	196
29	A Great Opportunity—Providentially Met	200
30	Severing Tender Ties	204

PUBLISHER'S FOREWORD

Many have called Arthur and Laura Carson "the apostles to the Chin people," but I am certain they would never have accepted such a lofty title. However, the amazing work this young dedicated couple did for the expansion of the Kingdom of God in Burma, and their many sacrifices, cannot be overstated. This first-hand account of their mission work, written by an aged Laura Carson who returned home several years after the death of her husband and remarried, offers a unique inside look at the difficult, yet inspiring, work of two of God's precious servants. The example of Laura Carson to young people, aspiring to apply themselves to the work of God, is priceless. Get this book into the hands of those who feel a calling to serve on the mission fields around the world or in their own back yards. The joy and determination of the Carsons in the face of great difficulty will have you holding your hand over your heart and giving thanks to God.

When I was writing *Myanmar Gold* to introduce the Christian world to a modern hero of the faith, my son Benjamin discovered this gem of a book while helping me do some research but could not find anywhere to purchase it. It was not only a valuable source for my project, it was a treasure we wanted others to be able to read. God used one of America's first foreign missionaries, the well-known Adoniram Judson, to begin His work in Burma in 1813, and it dovetailed beautifully into the work of the Carsons. The Carsons are still virtually unknown by most American Christians but beloved by their millions of spiritual children. Laura Hardin traveled to Burma in 1883 and was joined by Arthur Carson three years later. They were married the day he arrived in Burma. After three difficult years of ministry, the Carsons traveled deep into Burma's interior. When they arrived in Chin State, Burma in

1899, there were no indigenous Christians. Through their labors and those that followed after them, nearly ninety percent of an entire people group, the Chin (presently numbering nearly three million), now call themselves Christians. Because of harsh religious persecution in Burma, there are tens of thousands of Chin people around the world in communities in Indonesia, Australia, the United States, and other countries. Today, there are more than sixty Chin-affiliated churches in the United States. Some of them may be your neighbors. This is the story of how they came to Christ.

M. A. ROBINETTE
Foundations of Grace Publishing

INTRODUCTION

THE APOSTLES TO THE CHINS

In 1883 Laura Hardin was sent to Burma as a missionary under appointment by the Women's American Baptist Foreign Mission Society of the West, and assigned to work as teacher in the Mission School at Bassein.

Three years later she was married at Bassein to Rev. Arthur E. Carson, who had then just arrived from America under appointment by the American Baptist Missionary Union and designated for work among the Chins, being the first missionary sent to that people. After substituting for one year in Prome, while the missionary regularly assigned to that station was away on furlough, Mr. and Mrs. Carson established the first Chin Mission at Thayetmyo near the border between lower and upper Burma.

They acquired the language, secured a mission compound, erected buildings, established schools and churches; did some translating; carried on a persistent campaign of evangelism, touring a considerable district inhabited by Chins for that purpose.

This foundation work was continued with good success for ten years without interruption before a missionary was sent to relieve Mr. Carson for a furlough, long overdue.

After that furlough the Foreign Mission Board in response to the challenge of still more remote tribes of Chins, in the depths of paganism and degradation, unreached and untouched by any Christian message or influence, authorized the Carsons to advance the frontier of Christian work and influence back into the almost inaccessible hills of Upper Burma and establish a Mission among the semi-savage Chin tribes there.

This was nearly eighty-five years after Judson began his wonderful missionary work in Burma. But the soil to be cultivated was virgin soil, and the task not less difficult than that undertaken by the great first foreign missionary of our American Baptists. Although pagans, the Burmese, as Judson found them, at least had a language, a literature, a commerce and a civilization; but the remote hill tribes of Chins had none of these.

After a tour of this remote hill section and consultation with representatives of the English Government, which had come into control of that part of Burma only a few years before, Mr. Carson selected Haka as the strategic place in which to establish the new mission. The English Government had put a small military out-post there, and would not consent to the missionaries going to any place in that dangerous territory where there was no military post.

The long and dangerous journey to Haka, the difficulties of transporting to that remote and almost inaccessible fastness in the mountains, the necessary household goods and supplies for a year, the curiosity and inquisitiveness of the natives about seeing for the first time a white woman, the long efforts to overcome the suspicions and prejudices of uncivilized and savage tribes, and to acquire their strange unwritten languages under those conditions, are all depicted in this book with graphic vividness.

It is the romance of missions to carry civilization to uncivilized tribes, to create a written language for them, to translate the scriptures into their own dialect, to establish schools to educate their children, and hospitals to relieve their sufferings, to establish in the midst of their sordid and squalid living conditions, a real civilized Christian home, and to consecrate all these practical means and methods to the paramount purpose of winning them to Christ.

But it is a stupendous task and a long one. Judson found it so. Every foreign missionary the world around has found it so. The Carsons and their helpers (Karens who went with them to the Chin Hills) continued their arduous efforts six years before the first convert in the Haka District was baptized. Mr. Carson only lived and labored about three years after that, but he had the joy of baptizing the hundredth convert there before he was called to his reward in the Glory. At that time two dwellings and the hospital had been built on the Haka Compound; churches had been organized at Haka, Tiddim, and Lomban; schools conducted at Haka, Tiddim, Ktlan-Tlang, and Yokwa, one native preacher trained and several others in training.

Translations into Chin of Scripture passages, constituting the International Sunday School Lessons, had been made from week to week for several years, also Mrs. Judson's Catechism and forty-two hymns; and a systematic translation into Chin of the book of Matthew was almost complete.

It was while Mr. and Mrs. Carson were on a tour in a very remote part of the Haka district, ten days' hard travel from Haka, that he was stricken. With marvelous fortitude and wonderful endurance and vitality, they made their way back to Haka, where Dr. East operated for appendicitis. But the terrible strain of the long rough journey had drawn so heavily upon his splendid strength, that he only lived a day or two after the operation.

It was a great comfort to him in his dying hours to be assured that his devoted wife had no other thought than to carry on the work they had begun together. And this she did for twelve years and until her own health failed.

In the meantime Rev. J. Herbert Cope and his wife had come, and Mr. Cope had taken charge of the administrative work and the evangelistic work; Dr. and Mrs. East had been compelled to return to America; and Dr. J. G. Woodin and wife had come out to take their places; but later they also were compelled to leave the field.

Mrs. Carson, however, except while on furlough, carried on the school work, and the translation work, completing the book of Matthew and adding the other three gospels and the Acts in the Lai Chin language, also many gospel hymns; all of which were printed by the Mission Press at Rangoon. She prepared a Lai Chin Dictionary; she also maintained her home and as occasion required conducted church services, and devotional services, a daily clinic during the absence of the medical missionaries, and the administrative work during the absence of Mr. Cope, and in a very real sense she has been the "Mother" of the

Haka Mission; and the natives, both Christian and pagan, chiefs and common people, alike, so consider her and hold her in warmest love and devotion.

She left the work with deepest regret and her heart is still in it. But I am trying to convince her that the mission work to which the Lord has now assigned her, is to bring vision and inspiration to the home churches, so that the slump in missionary giving may be arrested, and our churches feel the responsibility and claim the privilege, of raising money enough, and sending men and women enough, to carry on the great work for which the way has been prepared by rare consecration and devotion and by the great sacrifices of the past.

In fact that is the chief purpose of the publishing of this book. When it was written, its primary purpose was to preserve for her sons and grandchildren, relatives and intimate friends, a record of the main events and incidents of a somewhat eventful life, as the frank intimacy of both the style and the matter indicates. Perhaps for that very reason the appeal to the denominational conscience will be more effective, because of admitting all the Baptist family to that same affectionate intimacy.

J. H. MERRIAM

PART I

ANTECEDENTS AND BEGINNINGS

CHAPTER I

FAMILY, CHILDHOOD, AND SCHOOL DAYS

My father, Evan Taylor Hardin, son of Asa and Elizabeth Hardin, was born near Frankfort, Kentucky. His father was a slave owner and planter. His mother, Elizabeth Taylor, was an own cousin to President Taylor. Both the Hardins and the Taylors were well-known, old aristocratic families of Kentucky. Asa Hardin was of the Hardin family, for which Hardin County was named, the county in which Abraham Lincoln was born.

My mother, Lentha Ames Boynton, was born in Windsor, Vermont. Her father's name was Levi Boynton, and her mother's name was Mary Griswold. Both father and mother died before she was five years old, and she was taken into the home of Abner Field and brought up as his daughter. There were three children in the Field family—Fred, Walbridge and Isadore—but the foster child always said that if there was any partiality shown in the family, by either father or mother, it was shown to her rather than to their own children, as, she was frail and delicate and their own children robust. Her cousin and foster brother Walbridge became Representative to Congress from Massachusetts, and afterwards was Chief Justice of the Supreme Court of Massachusetts for many years. Fred represented Springfield, Vermont, in the legislature twice and was afterwards senator from Windsor County. Lentha, though never a robust child, was carefully trained and was sent away to boarding school in Meridian, New Hampshire, and was given more education than was usually accorded to girls at that time. Her brother, Charles S. Boynton, went to try his fortune in the middle west, which was pioneer country at the time. He settled on a farm not far from Springfield, Illinois, in Sangamon County, and after a time wrote to his sister, Lentha, now eighteen, from whom we had been separated since childhood, and asked her to come west and keep house for him. This she consented to do. Meantime the slavery question was firing the hearts of people all over the country. When the agitation first began, Asa Hardin, one of the largest-hearted and most just men in the world, also owner of a large plantation and many slaves, decided that slave owning was wrong. He, therefore, seconded by his wife who was famous for her kindliness and sympathy, freed his slaves, thus relinquishing a fortune, sold his plantation and came north. He also settled in Sangamon County, Illinois, not far from Springfield and near the home of Charles Boynton.

At the time of the great gold excitement in 1849 Evan Hardin, son of Asa and Elizabeth Hardin, crossed the plains with ox teams to California. He had many hardships and narrow escapes from death by Indians, wild animals, and lack of water in "The Great American Desert." His brother was drowned in Feather River, and Evan took the remains East for burial—going via the Isthmus of Panama and overcoming almost insurmountable difficulties.

He returned to his father's home in Sangamon County, Illinois, and it was here that Evan Hardin and Lentha Boynton met and were later married. She was of Mayflower ancestry and had been brought up in accordance with the strictest New England Puritan rules and he with the warm-hearted, open-handed hospitality of the South. Although he proved to be of a roving disposition and found it hard to settle down to anything, he was one of the largest-souled men living and the union proved to be a very happy one.

The young couple went from Illinois to Fairfield, Iowa, where Mr. Hardin entered into the dry goods business with his brother-in-law. It was here that their first child, Charles Albert, was born. Mr. Hardin met with heavy losses because of his inability to "turn down" a friend. He signed a note for a considerable amount which he had to pay. As the money had to come out of the business, this angered his brother-in-law and led to their dissolving partnership.

Mr. Hardin then went to Harrison County (Iowa) to a small town north of Council Bluffs, called Calhoun. Here he bought property and again engaged in mercantile business. It was thought that Calhoun would become the large town of this vicinity and he refused to exchange lots there for those of equal size in what is now the heart of Omaha. But business proved slower than he had anticipated and, restless and eager to get on, he moved across the Missouri River to the little town of Coming City near the present location of Blair. During this residence in Calhoun, two sons were born to them—Abner Field in 1854, and George Nelson in 1856. In Coming City, September 28, 1858, I was born. My father had long wanted a daughter and was more than delighted to welcome me into his rapidly growing family.

I was given the name of Laurie Lentha. Later, when a school girl, I so disliked names ending in "ie" that I always wrote my name Laura. Then, when I married, not wishing to give up the family name of which I was unduly proud, I dropped the Lentha (from Lenthal, a surname in my mother's family) and retained the Hardin, and so have been Laura Hardin Carson since my marriage in 1886.

We lived in the midst of Winnebago Indians and were so annoyed by their begging and thieving that my mother was unwilling to remain among them. Accordingly, when I was two years old, my parents returned to Calhoun, where my father again engaged in the dry goods business. He seems to have prospered for a time for we owned and lived in the best house in town, and he carried on the leading business of the place. But he became interested in an "Iowa Swamp Land Investment Company," in which great fortunes were to be made. He invested all he had—and lost! He sold his store to meet outstanding debts—but he *did* meet them. He had barely enough left to buy a small farm of sixty acres about two miles out of town. My mother's jewels were traded for a small house which was moved to the farm and which for several years became my home.

While living in Calhoun a second daughter was born. As she was born on November 5, 1860, the day before Abraham Lincoln (who was a well-known and personal friend of my father's) was elected president, she was named Julia Lincoln.

Soon after this time came the civil war. My father heard the call of his country and was among the first to volunteer for service. He belonged to the 29th Regiment, Company A, Iowa Volunteers (Infantry). My brave, courageous, and patriotic mother, although in frail health and with five small children, no money and nothing else, except a miserable house of four rooms and sixty acres of land, made no complaint, but encouraged my father's volunteering. His brother, John J. Hardin of Springfield, Illinois (and long afterwards county treasurer of Sangamon County), whose sympathies were with the South, wrote such scathing letters with regard to the matter that it led to an estrangement which lasted for many years after the war had ended.

Though less than four years old at the time, I well remember the morning my father left for the war. My oldest brother, Charles, was then nine years old. My father charged him so tenderly and earnestly with the care of my mother that the tears streamed down her cheeks, and my heart was filled with wonder as to what it all meant, as my father, after kissing the others good-by, lifted me from the highchair and pressed me to his breast.

There are a few things indelibly silhouetted against the sky of my memory that were impressed upon my childish mind during those awful days of war. My father always, if possible, wrote to my mother immediately before and after a battle. I can remember her, after putting us children to bed, walking the floor and wringing her hands in anguish.

I could not understand what it meant then, but I have thought since it was times when she was waiting for the letter after the battle. Poor Mother! How bravely she fought with poverty, want and anxiety during those years, no one will ever know. But she was a good mother. Her boys were well trained, strong and obedient and were a great help and comfort to her.

I remember that we were obliged to eat corn bread and molasses or go hungry—for there was nothing else. I was inclined to be delicate as a little child, and the corn bread did not agree with me. Because there was nothing else, and I was obliged to eat it, it threw me into dysentery and I was very ill. My mother felt that she *must* get me some wheat bread or lose me. There was no flour to be had; but there was an old flour mill about five miles distant that had not been running for many months. One night my mother put the younger children to bed, and with the two older boys for company and to carry the grain, walked to Hardy's mill on Willow Creek, and getting Judge Hardy out of bed, told him her pitiful story, beseeching him to grind enough of the wheat, which the boys carried, to keep her child from dying. Judge Hardy was a kindly man and was deeply touched. He said the mill was not in grinding order, but that he would try the next day to put it in shape to grind her little bit of wheat, and would send her the flour. I do not remember whether the flour came or not; but I do remember how she was buoyed up with the hope of getting it. I remember also her sending the boys on a five-mile tramp to the home of a distant cousin of my father's (Rebecca Mathews) to tell her of our need and to ask her, if possible, to obtain a loaf of white bread for us. I can never forget when the boys came home bringing a huge, brown loaf of fresh, white bread. I think nothing in all the years since has ever looked quite so good to me as that beautiful loaf of white bread—which probably saved my life.

Our house was very open and cold—snow sifted through the cracks upon our beds in winter, and fuel was almost unobtainable. My mother did not know how we were to get through the winter. Often, month after month passed by without her receiving, until long after due, the pittance of my father's pay. The struggles with poverty during those days were hard, indeed. Finally a kind man, Harris Day, who could not get into the army because of lameness, who had a good wife, a large house, and no children, learning of my mother's brave struggles, came and offered to give us rooms in his house and to furnish us with plenty of fuel for the winter, as a small part of his duty to his country. My mother shrank from being a burden to others, but was finally obliged to accept the kind offer. I remember being there during the winter and the great kindness of Mr. and Mrs. Day to my mother and especially to us children. The boys went to school and Mr. Day made prairie-chicken traps for them which were placed near a large pile of sugar-cane seed. The snow was deep and continuous that winter and the prairie-chickens came in large numbers to feed on the cane seed, and the boys caught dozens of them for market and for food, so the enterprise proved a great blessing to us.

I do not know just how long we stayed there but one little incident which I well remember shows the kind consideration of Mr. Day. He had a niece who was a school teacher, a Miss Walden, who sometimes came to her uncle's for the week-end. She was very fond of little children and on the occasions of these visits used to ask me to sleep with her. One night, after putting me to bed, some company came in, and she left me. The bed was near a wall and in tumbling about, I struck my foot against the window and broke to atoms a pane of glass. I was terrified at what I had done. I knew that my mother had no money. What would she say? What would she do? Perhaps the glass was not badly broken and if only I could get it, perhaps I could fit the pieces in. But I could not raise the sash and I could not get out of doors to see without going through the room where the company was. I spent a half hour of anguish and finally decided to go through the room very quietly and slip out of doors and examine the broken glass. So, in my nighty, and feeling very guilty, and as if nothing but the gallows would do for me if I could not restore the glass, I glided quietly through the room, receiving many pleasant smiles from the guests as I did so. It was very cold, my feet were bare, and the glass was in atoms. I soon slipped back to bed, but not to sleep, feeling that my doom was near. When the guests were gone, Miss Walden came in, noticed the broken window and went out again. Presently Mr. Day called me, and feeling myself the most awful culprit imaginable, I went out to him.

He took me in his arms and asked, "Did you break the window?" "Yes, but it is broken all in little pieces, and I could not put them back," I said, beginning to cry. "Never mind, little girl. Accidents will happen. I will forgive you if you won't tell your mother. You must say nothing about it to her," he said, kissing me and sending me back to bed. Few times in my life can I remember ever having felt so great a sense of relief. To be forgiven and not even have to tell my mother about it! It seemed too good to be true. The kind-hearted man felt that my mother had troubles enough and did not want her worried over the broken glass.

In the spring we went back to the farm; for the boys must till the land though they had only an ox team with which to do it. The place was run down and the fence partly gone, but they worked like Trojans, for were they not to do *the work of men* while their father was fighting for his country?

I do not remember much that transpired during that summer—the second year of the war—but one incident seems ineffaceably stamped upon my memory. For several weeks Father had been lying very ill in the hospital at Little Rock, Arkansas. The troops were suddenly moved from there. He was too ill to be moved and was left among the dead and dying. One of those angels of mercy, an army nurse, came through, found that he was still alive and tenderly ministered to him until he was able to travel. She then procured a ten days' furlough for him and sent him home to his loved ones.

One evening almost at sunset, we were all standing in the yard when Mother, shading her eyes with her hand, and looking intently up the road in the direction of the glowing sunset, said, "I declare! There comes a man who walks like your Father. I do believe... Yes! It is! *It is he!* Come on!" and we all fairly flew to the arms of the man who was hurrying in our direction. What a meeting that was, and what a parting ten days later! We had heard that he was very ill from a letter written by a comrade before the troops were moved. That letter was followed by weeks of silence, and Mother had almost given him up for dead and was living in anguish, watching hourly for official news of him.

The furlough was soon over and we were alone again with another winter to face. It was that winter, I think, that we moved back to Calhoun and lived in "the little red house under the hill." Mother could not bear that her children should not be in school, and she probably moved there so that the younger ones, for whom it was too far to walk in winter from the farm, could have the advantages of school. The house also was warmer and fuel was very scarce and hard to get. In that part of the country coal had never yet been used for fuel and the able-bodied men all having gone to war, it was next to impossible to get sufficient wood hauled from the timber. On Saturdays the boys would yoke up the ox team in the morning, go to the woods and bring back enough wood to last until the next Saturday. This would take them practically the whole day; and only by the strictest economy could the wood be made to keep our fire going for a week.

I do not remember many things that transpired during that winter. One thing I do remember is that the Winnebago Indians camped near our place and had to pass our house when going to and from town. Although, when sober, they were friendly and harmless except for thieving, when filled with "firewater" they not infrequently took advantage of there being no men about, and committed such depredations that women and children were in terror at sight of them. One afternoon Mother received a letter from Father. The letter contained news of Captain Danielson, father of the girl that my brother, Field, afterwards married. Mother cautioned us children not to go out of the yard, saying there were drunken Indians in town, and that she would be back in a few moments. She took the letter to hurry with the news to Mrs. Danielson. When she returned a half hour later, the Indians had taken possession of the house, one was lying drunk under the bed and we children were screaming with terror. Fortunately, Mother had with her a dog of which the Indians were greatly afraid. He growled so savagely at them that when Mother told them that she would let him after them if they did not leave immediately they got their drunken companion on his feet and hustled away. The absolute terror I experienced on that occasion I shall never forget.

On December 13th of that hard winter my brother, Evan Shelby, was born, making six children for my poor mother to care for. Many times when she was too ill to be up and about the house, I can remember her sitting up in bed, cutting and making garments for us. It was before the days of readymade clothing for children, and at that time a sewing machine was a great curiosity. She had none, and every garment for all six children had to be made by hand. But the months dragged by and at last came news of Lee's surrender. The awful war was over and my father came home. We went back to the farm, the boys tilled the ground as best they could with our ox team, and Father worked at the "cabinet maker's" trade, but he was much broken in health and it was all he could do to supply us with absolute necessities. The boys were good and obedient, with no bad habits, but were still but children. Those were hard years while we children were growing up, and two more little ones came into the family while we were on the farm after my father's return from the war—Harriet Emily (Emma) and Robert Clarence.

We older children went to the school in Calhoun where all grades were taught by one teacher. My older brothers were frequently obliged to get work, to help support the family. As I grew older there was seldom a week that I was not kept at home at least one or two days to help Mother, whose health was always delicate. Finally I stayed out of school altogether and worked very hard. Before I was thirteen I did practically all of the washing and ironing for our large family, besides doing a considerable part of the housework. It took most of Mother's time to do the sewing, as we children were older and she made all of the suits for the boys as well as clothes for herself and us girls. About this time my father bought her a sewing machine—a "Weed." It was the second one I had ever seen. Needless to say, it facilitated the sewing greatly—especially as my oldest brother learned to operate it and was glad to help Mother whenever at leisure to do so.

We children attended Sunday School in the only church in the place—the Methodist. There was a very small library of old-fashioned Sunday School books. I brought one home one day, a Missionary book which had pictures of the hideous idols in India and told how the people worshiped them instead of the Christ whom we knew and loved. I took the book to Mother and asked her if the things in it were really true. She said that they were, and talked of our duty to those who did not even know that God so loved the world that He gave his only-begotten son that whosoever believeth in Him should not perish but have everlasting life. The talk and the pictures made an impression on me that I never forgot and were the beginning of my interest in missions. I said then, "When I get an education, I would like to go and teach them." But my chance for an education seemed remote enough—though there were influences at work of which I knew nothing.

Joining our farm on the east there was a nursery owned by a man who had an only daughter, named Ella, who was my closest, most devoted friend and classmate. Her parents were fine people. When she was thirteen years old (I was six months older), they decided to send her to the Magnolia High School, recently founded at Magnolia, Iowa, and presided over by an unusually fine teacher, Professor J. D. Hornby. Ella besought me to try to induce my parents to let me go with her. Though I longed to go with an inexpressible longing, I felt that the matter was hopeless and refused to mention the subject to my people. Finally Mr. and Mrs. Day, Ella's parents, came one evening and talked the matter over with my father and mother, saying that if I did not go then, in all probability I would never go to school any more; for when older even if there were opportunity, I would probably be ashamed to go into classes with children much younger than myself; then they felt that I was working much too hard for a young girl, which it would be very difficult to avoid if I remained at home; and lastly they could not bear to have Ella and me separated. They said they had been to Magnolia, had made inquiries and had found a place for Ella to board where the people would be willing to take me to work for my board if my parents would allow me to go. They talked the matter over privately for a long time. Finally, I was amazed when they told me they had decided to let me go. It seemed too good to be true; but my joy was tempered by the thought that I ought not to leave my mother with burdens of work far beyond what I knew she was able to carry. My sister, Julia, two years younger than myself, hated housework, but she was willing to do any out-door work that she was called upon to do, and she loved Mother enough to overcome her dislike for housework, and came splendidly to the rescue after I was gone.

In September, 1872, when I was fourteen years old, I went with Ella to Magnolia and we entered school together. We lived with Mrs. A. N. Oviatt, Ella as a boarder and I working for my board, my father paying only for my music lessons. He was inordinately fond of music and one of his fondest hopes was that his oldest daughter should be a musician. Mrs. Oviatt was a fine music teacher, and he hoped that this would be my opportunity. But in this he was destined to bitter disappointment, for I never had a note of music in me that I was capable of expressing, though I have sometimes felt that like Trilby's manager, there was marvelous music *in my soul*, if only I could find expression for it. But I failed to find it in my dear "Aunt Nean's" old piano. To my dying day I shall never forget how I watched the clock the hours I had to practice. I feel bound to say, however, that I think I could have learned to play a little, very mechanically, had not my brothers made so much fun of my miserable attempts that I always thought that I was doing really worse than I was. Having three older brothers, frank as brothers usually are, I was not allowed to grow vain along any lines. I well remember my brother, George, planting himself in front of me and, with head to one side and hands on hips, recounting my beauties as follows: "redheaded, freckled-faced, snubnosed, snaggle-toothed, left-handed, big-footed, *fat!*" And the evident disgust with which he enumerated these qualities pierced me to the soul. I felt as though it was almost a crime to have red hair; and what I suffered from being called "Carrots," "Sorrel Top," and so forth, no one except a child with a very sensitive nature can know. It therefore took actual suffering from my young life when Aunt Nean (Mrs. Oviatt) pronounced my hair very beautiful, and did the work herself that I should have done, in order to brush my red-gold hair around her finger into conventional curls, mornings before I went to school. Up to this time I believed that I was the embodiment of all that was ugly and awkward and inefficient. Looking back from this distance, I believe that I was an ordinary-looking girl with freckled face, fair clear complexion, snub-nose and plump body. If I had any beauty at all, it was my clear, fair skin and my hair. I was only a mediocre student with ordinary ability, but I had a great longing always to make something worthwhile of my life. It was in Magnolia High School that I first met Newell Dwight Hillis, who years afterwards was a strong factor in making me believe it possible for me to prepare for foreign mission service. One of his sisters died, and, on the day of her funeral, another sister left from the cemetery on her journey as a missionary to Ceylon. This made a profound impression on me and I secretly resolved that some day I would go to teach those who had not the knowledge of salvation through Jesus Christ.

During my second year in Magnolia, my father decided that he must make more effort to provide for his three large boys who were rapidly growing into men. There was much talk at the time of opportunities opening in western Nebraska for farm homesteads. Good farms were to be had for living upon and improving them. My oldest brother, Charles, was much interested; and encouraged by my father, he engaged to go out to Furnas County with Mr. George Sayers, a well-to-do Englishman who became one of the first settlers on Medicine Creek, north of the present town of Cambridge. Charles was much pleased with the prospects and filed on a quarter section of land which had an abundance of both wood and water. As the nearest railroad was more than fifty miles distant, it was impossible to get lumber for building purposes even if money had been available. Both Mr. Sayers and Charles *dug* rather than built their homes. Excavations were made into a bank, then walls of sod were built up for two or three feet above the ground so that windows could be put in. On these walls a framework of poles was made for a roof; this framework was covered with brush, then a layer of sod was put on and the whole covered with earth. It is true these roofs sometimes leaked, but not often—rain was woefully infrequent!

I remember, however, hearing my husband tell of two Baptist ministers coming out from the East and being entertained in his father's "dugout," as these dwellings were called. In the middle of the night there came a torrential rain and muddy water streamed through the roof. He went out to see how the guests were faring and found one of them sitting up in bed wearing his silk (stovepipe) hat and holding his umbrella over it for protection. Needless to say that on the following day he "struck the trail," hat intact, for the East and never to return!

Charles finished his dugout and found it warm and comfortable. He wrote glowing accounts of fine land to be secured for the taking and urged my father to sell the little farm, put the money into good cows and come before the best land had all been taken by others. Accordingly, the farm was sold, the cows bought, and all of our earthly belongings not otherwise disposed of were packed into two covered wagons, one of which was drawn by horses and the other by oxen, and the journey from Harrison County, Iowa, to Furnas County, Nebraska, was begun. Just how long it took us, I do not now remember; but to the younger members of the party, each day was full of interest and delight as we plodded along, driving our cows or riding in the covered wagons and camping nights. Oh, the fragrance of the coffee and bacon over those camp fires! I can smell it yet.

My sixteenth birthday was celebrated on the trip at Lone Tree (now Central City), Nebraska.

Sometime in October, 1874, we reached the little log postoffice and trading post, Medicine Creek, which was at that time the only building in the place. The postmaster kept a few supplies which he freighted across the country from Plum Creek—now Lexington—on the Union Pacific Railway. Times were so hard in the vicinity during those first years that the Post was dubbed by the settlers as "Scratchpot" and by this name it became known all over the country, until later, when the railroad came through, it was given the more euphonious name of Cambridge.

We settled for the winter in my brother Charles' dugout, while my father began the search for a suitable home for us. This he eventually found on the south side of the Republican River about three miles from Cambridge. He bought a hundred and sixty acres of land with a two-room house (hewed log—with an upper room or attic which was reached by a ladder), a good pump and a few other improvements upon it. In payment for this he turned in a large percentage of our little herd of cows. We were to have possession in the spring. Never shall I forget the winter spent in the Medicine Creek dugout. My father and brother went to Plum Creek and laid in a store of flour, a little sugar, coffee, salt, etc.—just barest necessities. With our cows, which had the rich buffalo grass that covered the ground at that time and made the best of winter pasture, we had plenty of milk and butter. But there were months on end when we had absolutely nothing to eat but the delicious cream toast which my mother was so skillful in making. There were no vegetables and no meat—just a little dried fruit or dried corn at long intervals for an especial treat. My father felt that we must have a greater variety of food to retain health, so he and my brother joined some buffalo hunters—men who hunted buffaloes for their robes, which they hauled to Plum Creek or some other railroad town and exchanged for provisions, ammunition and clothing. The plains were covered in those days with great herds of buffaloes; and for years afterwards their bleaching bones whitened the plains in every direction.

It did not take the hunters long to secure and market their load of robes; but somehow they missed the herd they expected to find on their way home and came in without meat. We children were greatly disappointed for we were so hungry for meat! The buffaloes did not usually come very close to the settlement. But one morning a herd was sighted not far away and my father and brother were soon after them. They killed eleven that morning before breakfast. A wagon was taken out to the hunting ground and a whole load of hams, humps, loin roasts, and tongues—only the choicest parts—were brought home. My! How we feasted! A little house was made out of brush where the meat could be kept frozen and we had no lack of animal food during the rest of the winter.

I remember that winter as one of the most carefree of my life. My brother owned a pony team and a spring wagon. With only two rooms, without floors, little to cook, and nothing to sew, there was little to keep two girls full of life and spirit indoors. We learned to ride and drive the ponies. Almost daily we either rode or drove to the postoffice, three and one-half miles away, for the mail. We became so expert at driving, always taking turns, that we became very proud of our horsemanship. We actually practiced driving around the head of a deep ravine to see how near we could drive to the edge of the cliff without going over. But one day, when the hind wheel did practically go over, we were terrified enough to make us stop such foolhardy performances. We were not agreed, however, as to which was the better driver—the one who came closest to the edge without going over, or the one who went practically over, yet came out of the scrape without accident. All cowboys in the country had nice riding ponies, and we girls had frequent opportunities to ride them. We were not afraid to mount anything that our brothers would permit us to mount, and many were the gay rides we had that our parents knew nothing about. Riding was the only amusement there was at that time for young people except the settlement dances. My parents had never approved of dancing, but they hadn't the heart to forbid us attending these, cut off as we were from all other social life. The settlers were for the most part uneducated and uncouth, but almost universally warm-hearted, honest and kind. There were a few who felt keenly the lack of school and religious advantages. Some of these got together in the spring of 1875 and organized a union Sunday School. Mr. S. K. Keyes, as I remember it, was superintendent. The Sunday School was held in a little one-room log cabin without any floor. Some of the people brought chairs and a few planks from their homes and planks placed on chairs formed the seats. I was asked to take a class of small boys. I took them into one corner and taught them most enthusiastically. One small boy, son of the superintendent, sat directly in front of me and gazed up into my face with apparently rapt interest. I was flattered, feeling sure that one boy at least was drinking in all I said and would be good all the rest of his life. The lesson ended. The room was quiet. "Would any boy like to ask a question?" I asked, smiling into the upturned face before me. Quick as a flash—"Teacher, *what makes your nose kick up so?*" came back at me from the admiring boy. I giggled. Everybody in the room heard and roared, so that it was impossible for me to give even my brother George's explanation, that it was to hang my dinner pail on when I went to school. That was the beginning of my religious work, and I felt somewhat chagrined.

That spring we moved to my father's farm south of the river, into the log house to which two sod rooms had been added. This was at that time the best house in the entire settlement—in fact the only one with a shingled roof and there were shingles only over the log part of this house.

A part of the land had been under cultivation a year or two but was still new and rich. More was plowed and all was planted. It was a good year and crops enormous. Finer corn one would not wish to see than grew that year in Republican Valley, and hopes ran high. But, alas! they were not long-lived. Long before the fields of splendid corn were mature, there came one bright cloudless day a dark shadow over the sun and presently there descended upon the earth myriads and myriads of grasshoppers or locusts. They attacked every living thing in the way of vegetable matter, taking every leaf as they went. In three or four hours, there was nothing left of the magnificent corn fields except the bare stalks about a foot above the ground.

Every leaf was taken from the trees and everything that resembled vegetation from the garden. The windows were darkened by the pests and on the sides of the house they were so thick you could not put down the end of a cane without touching one. The following day, when everything was gone, they suddenly rose, again darkened the sun, and traveled on, leaving nothing but desolation behind them. This devastation made the winter indescribably hard for the settlers. Again we were without vegetables. We had a fine lot of young hogs, but now there would be no corn to feed them. My father and brother killed them and cured the meat. Taking ours, and buying a load from one of our neighbors, they started over the plains to the Black Hills. It was at the time of the gold excitement there and they hoped to dispose of the meat at a good price. My father also hoped that his experience in the early days in California might lead him into something good from the mines. But vain were all their hopes. They returned after three or four months, not having made enough to pay for the meat bought of the neighbor, and my brother having contracted mountain fever from which he never recovered.

One day, as my seventeenth birthday was drawing near, the school director called at our house. He surprised me by saying, "We want you to teach our school this winter." "Why, I don't know enough to teach school," I replied. "Well, we have got to have a school and you will have to teach it. I guess you have had more schooling than any of the rest of the youngsters anyhow, and you must do what you can for them," he replied. And so it was arranged that I was to teach the school—the second term ever taught in the district—*if I could get a certificate*. I had very grave doubts of being able to secure one. The County Superintendent lived some twenty-five miles distant, and it was arranged that my brother Field should take the ponies and spring wagon and drive me to his home where I would take the examination and return the next day. The long drive in the cold, raw wind gave me a raging headache. It was evening when we got there. After supper and a cup of tea, I took the examination, which I suspect the Superintendent made rather easy for me. Anyhow, wonder of wonders, I got my certificate! I returned home triumphant and happy.

That winter I shall always remember as one of the hardest of my life. My mother was in miserable health. My two brothers and two sisters then at home all went to school to me. We had to walk more than two miles. That winter the snow was very deep and the cold intense. I arose long before daylight and prepared breakfast, while my sister Julia helped with the milking. We washed the dishes, put the house in order and put up lunch for five of us before starting on our two miles' tramp through the snow.

There were some grown boys in school older by several years than I was. One was a fine mathematician. Nobody will ever know how hard I worked to keep ahead of him that winter. Mentally it was good for me, but with all the physical strain added, I realized that I could not keep up the pace another year. My sister and I were obliged to do the family washing and ironing evenings and Saturdays, and often after washing I sat up until far into the night working over the arithmetic problems which must be taught the next day. My mother realized that it was too hard for me and encouraged me to go to Illinois to the home of her brother and attend school the following year. Not far from Pleasant Plains there was an excellent country school, known as Franklin Academy, which my cousins attended. I wrote my uncle of my desire to teach and of the need of further education. He replied very cordially, inviting me to come and spend the winter in his home and go to school with his daughter who really needed the company of an older girl.

CHAPTER 2

CONVERSION AND PIONEER HARDSHIPS

During the winter of my first school teaching—1875—there came an evangelist from our county seat and held Revival Meetings in the old sod school house where I taught. Practically everybody in the community attended, and many were converted. I was a leader among the young people. Many watched and waited for me to make a start. I was adamant. The preacher talked to me about how many I was holding back from the way of salvation. I made no reply, though the thought of my responsibility for others gave me many wakeful nights. My brother Charles to whom I was devotedly attached, begged me to yield to the pleadings of Christ and seek eternal salvation. My mother spoke to me very lovingly and tenderly. She said all the rest of the family had chosen the better way and it would break her heart if I did not go with them. I made no reply, but I was very miserable. I had made up my mind that I would never, never ask for prayers or say publicly that I wanted to be a Christian. The fact was I danced. I was fascinated with dancing. Christians thought it was wrong. It was *not* wrong, and I was not going to give it up. I would dance as much as I liked. I would also live such a model Christian life that people couldn't help seeing that my influence was better than that of those who were joining the church—even though *they* didn't dance.

Days and nights went by. Oh, such days, such miserable days and nights for me. I doubt if ever anybody felt a deeper sense of sin, or a stronger determination never to confess it before men. Finally, the night before the meetings were to close, when the invitation was given, before I realized what I was doing, involuntarily I was on my feet. It seemed as if a power I could not control prompted me. I wanted to be disgusted and ashamed of my weakness, but the sense of relief was so great I was filled with rejoicing. If I had been miserable before, I was blissfully, radiantly happy now. The thought of dancing, which had held me back for so long, lost all attraction for me. My mind and heart were filled with higher, holier things. Oh, there was so much to be done in the world to bring the great over-mastering joy I had found into the hearts of others! What sacrifice was it to give up dancing? I hated the thought of having allowed so insignificant a thing to have kept me away from Christ. I sought eagerly for worth-while things to do. My mother had a number of old-fashioned religious books. They had never had the least interest for me before. I now read with avidity everything of the kind I could lay hands on and longed for more. The wish to be a foreign missionary, long dormant (for it would never do for a missionary to dance), now revived. However, it would take a thorough education to become a missionary and I knew that the only hope of an education was to earn it through my own work. Up to this time I had spent my earnings, in so far as I could, to add a few comforts—bare necessities really—to the home.

Soon after my conversion, a Methodist Church and Sunday School were organized in my little sod school house—now "Sunny Hillside." Nearly all of the new converts went into these organizations, including my brother Charles who became Superintendent of the Sunday School. I became a teacher in the Sunday School and was truly and deeply sorry that I could not become a member of the Methodist Church. The Evangelist labored with me, urging that I would keep others from joining. I told him that if he could prove to me from the Bible that infant baptism was taught there, I would not hesitate a moment. He said as a matter of fact he did not believe much in infant baptism himself, that he had never had his own little children baptized, preferring to wait until they were old enough to realize what they were doing. "And yet you practice it," I said, "practice what you don't believe in. I could not do that, neither could I say, through the church to the world, that I believe in it when in my heart I do not," and there the matter dropped.

In the autumn of that year I went to my uncle's (Charles S. Boynton), near Pleasant Plains, Illinois, and attended the Franklin School.

My cousin Ella and I usually rode the same horse, one behind the other. In the winter when the mud was thin and deep and the horse broke through the ice with every step we sometimes felt that it was getting an education under difficulties. But the fact that we *were* getting an education meant much to me. The school was a good one and for me it was a wonderful opportunity. My uncle was "well-to-do" and highly respected in the community. Both he and his wife were very kind to me. They were prominent members of the Baptist Church in Berlin. My uncle was a deacon, greatly beloved, who was always in his place in church. I regularly attended church with them. We had three or four miles to drive, but no matter how bad the roads—and often our carriage wheels would block full of the thick clay—we were always there.

That winter the church called a new pastor, a young man just fresh from the Seminary—Lee M. Goff. This was his first pastorate and I was the first person he ever baptized.

I remained at my uncle's until the end of the school year, then returned to Nebraska, where I again engaged in teaching. I was made Superintendent of the Sunday School. Being deeply interested in religious things I tried with some degree of success to influence my pupils to Christian living. This encouraged me to once more seriously consider foreign missions; and I prayed that God would help me to know his will in the matter.

About this time I was visited by a school director from Lynden (now Hendley) and was offered a better salary than they were able to pay in our home district. My brothers and sisters accused me of being a little hard on them in my anxiety not to seem partial. I was therefore glad to try a new district and contracted for the school.

When our own director learned of it he was much disappointed and immediately made arrangements to send his oldest son to the district to which I was going in order that he might continue under my instruction. As he was a prominent man and represented more money than all the rest of the community, at that time, his practical approval of me in this way materially added to my reputation as a teacher. It was while teaching here in a little log house and boarding with a German family in a three-roomed dugout that I first met Arthur Carson.

He had come with his parents to seek a home on the western prairies. He was the oldest of three sons. His father was partially paralyzed and had to walk with crutches, so upon Arthur's young shoulders came the responsibilities of the family when he was only eighteen years old. There were two younger brothers and one sister in the family, besides his parents.

He was graduated from the Morning Sun (Iowa) High School before starting for the West and had taught one term of school. He was converted while quite a young man and had united with the Baptist Church.

After coming to Nebraska, the Carsons settled near the place I was teaching and Arthur taught in an adjoining district. It was during this time that there began a friendship between us that culminated in our marriage, on the other side of the world, many years later.

The year of my return from Illinois was fraught with incidents not soon to be forgotten. There were continued rumors of Indian depredations to the west of us. Finally there came authentic news of the raiding of a settlement where houses had been looted, cattle and ponies driven away, and about thirty settlers had been killed. One brave woman, alone in a dugout, with a good rifle and plenty of ammunition, had kept them at bay for five hours when the approach of some cowboys caused the few remaining Indians to flee. The whole settlement presented a scene of utter desolation. Houses had been pillaged and burned, featherbeds ripped open and their contents scattered to the four winds, stock driven away and inhabitants killed.

As this all happened only about thirty or forty miles west of us, naturally the people in our settlement felt nervous and uneasy.

One morning a month or so after this news had reached us, there came madly riding into our dooryard, the foam flying from the sides of his panting pony as he rode, a man, who only halted long enough to call out, "The Indians are upon us—only a few miles away—hurry to Medicine Creek (Post) at once for protection," and he rode wildly on to warn other settlers. My father, who had had plenty of experience fighting Indians while crossing the plains, soon had the boys driving cows, harnessing horses, etc., while he looked after firearms and ammunition, and Mother and we girls got together such provisions and bedding as we could and loaded them into the wagon. We all worked feverishly, and when preparations were finished and loads of people with their belongings were hurrying from every direction to the Post, my father urged us to hurry and get into the wagon. I said very quietly, "Go on, I am not going."

"You are not going!" said my father, "and why not?"

"I am not afraid," I said, "and I would rather stay here than be in the mob. If the Indians come, they will see the place is deserted and I can easily hide."

Without a word, my father put down his gun and sat down. When I urged him to go he said, "What kind of a father would I be to leave a young girl here to face marauding Indians alone?"

Without further protest, I climbed into the wagon with the others, and started for the Post, but only once in after life can I remember ever being compelled to do anything that went so against the grain; and that happened in the far-away Chin Hills more than forty years later.

It was indeed a mob that gathered at the Post. Rapidly some organization was made and leaders appointed. All ponies, horses and cattle were put together and men in relays appointed to herd them day and night, not far from camp. Lookouts were appointed and signals agreed upon. A stockade was made of the wagons inside of which the women and children were to be kept. Beeves were killed for food and the meat parceled out to the mothers of families who cooked it over camp-fires. Beds were made under the wagons on the ground. In this stockade and in this way we lived for two days and nights. On the second day I secretly slipped put to the herd, caught a pony, mounted it and rode home, a distance of about three miles, alone. I fed and watered the chickens, looked about to see that nothing had been disturbed and returned to banter the herders for allowing a pony to be taken without their knowledge. When my mother learned of my escapade she was justly indignant and gave me what I deserved in the way of reproof.

On the third day of our stockade experience, scouts returned with the news that the Indians "unmistakably seen" had proved to be a band of cowboys taking a small bunch of cattle north. Upon receipt of this news, we all returned to our homes, but not without some thrilling experiences, for there were false alarms a time or two which filled the camp with terror and panic.

Later in the autumn of the same year the whole country was devastated by prairie fires. These were supposed by many to have been set by Indians, in revenge for the depredations made by hunters upon the rapidly disappearing herds of buffaloes. Be that as it may, I have never seen such desolation as reigned in the Republican Valley after being swept by these fires.

One day my father and brother were going to town in the spring wagon. My mother and I persuaded them to take us about three miles west to the home of a cousin, before crossing the river, leave us there for a visit and return for us toward evening. The cousin was living in a new sod house. He had threshed his grain and there were large stacks of straw south of the house, also a large pile of wood that had been hauled for the winter. It was nearly noon when we arrived, and my father and brother were persuaded to stay until after dinner before going on to town. Accordingly they unhitched their horses and tied them in the straw-roofed barn while they came in to dinner. Shortly before dinner my father called our attention to the hazy condition of the atmosphere and remarked that there must be a prairie fire not far away. My brother went to the door and looked out, remarking that it was getting very smoky and he thought he would ride to the top of the "bench" and see if he could locate the fire. He soon returned saying that he could see nothing of the fire and he thought it must be beyond Beaver Creek, more than fifteen miles away. Almost immediately we sat down to dinner, father facing the window to the south. Before halfway through the meal he jumped from his chair, crying, "The fire is upon us, come quick!" My cousin and brother followed him, running to the barns which were already on fire. They drew and opened their knives as they ran, cut the halters of the horses in the barn and drove the terrified creatures toward plowed ground. They let down the sides of the hog pen and tried to save the hogs. My father and brother saw it was no use. They were so stifled by the heat and smoke that they made a mad rush for the house, realizing that it were better to save themselves than the pigs.

In trying to rescue the poor perishing animals, my cousin's hands were frightfully burned and his way to the house was cut off by the flames. Bethinking himself of a new well not yet finished he ran and dropped himself into it until the fire had passed. While this was going on outside, what of us inside? The house being built and covered with new sod, we at first thought ourselves perfectly secure from personal danger. But we soon had reason to change our minds. The stacks and woodpile burning so near made the heat and smoke so intense that we gasped for breath. The flames shot in about the poles that supported the roof and clothing hanging on the walls caught fire. The well not yet being finished, water was hauled for use from the river. There was a barrelful just outside the door. We brought bucketful after bucketful and put out the flames as clothing and bedding ignited. I had not the least hope of ever escaping from that house alive. The glass in the windows was glowing red, the smoke and the heat was suffocating. My mother said quite calmly that we must prepare for death. She prayed for my little eight-year-old brother, who had been left to herd the cattle, and for my sister at home alone. What would be their fate? Our hearts stood still as we thought of them.

Almost as suddenly as the fire had come upon us, it passed over. The wind was terrific and carried it with such force that burning bark was blown clear across the Republican River and fire caught on the north side. With the lessening of the heat and clearing of smoke, my father, cousin and brother rushed on to help the neighbors, many of whom were losing all they had. As soon as I dared, I begged mother to allow me to start for home. I longed yet dreaded to know the worst. I had not a doubt but that everything we had would be in ashes. Oh, if only the lives of the dear ones were spared, I would ask no more. I flew over the road, frequently stepping into fire, my feet burning and my shoes shriveling with the heat, and every breath a prayer.

I tore past homes that were in flames, saw the carcasses of domestic animals lying charred on the prairie and great piles of roasting, smoldering grain from around which the granaries had been burned. But I could not stop for anything, for oh, my brother and sister! Where were they? What had been their fate? I rushed on as fast as my burning feet would carry me. No one could ever put into words the sense of relief that came over me when I saw that our house, the only one with a shingle roof, floors, and log walls in the neighborhood, was still standing. I stopped to thank God and take breath and then rushed on.

I found my sister all right and my brother also. It seemed almost too good to be true. My sister saw the fire coming and rushed the calves and hogs out of the pens into a plowed field. The fire came within a short distance from the house when the wind suddenly changed and it was saved. My little brother saw the fire coming. Fortunately he was herding his cattle near the river. He realized the danger, young as he was, and rushed his herd into the middle of the broad, shallow stream. He said when the heat and smoke got so bad he could not stand it he ducked his head under water. We were up all that night fighting fire. Wind swirled sparks into the straw-covered sheds and barn and they were partly burned. While pumping water to help save them my own clothes caught fire at the back and were badly burned when my brother, coming for the water I was pumping, caught sight of them in time to extinguish the flames before I was aware of their burning. We were so surrounded by heat and smoke and fire that, as I think of it now, it seems only by the mercy of God that any of us escaped with our lives.

The next morning when the fire was over and the wind had abated, the country presented such an aspect of desolation as I have never witnessed before or since. That winter is one long to be remembered by the people who lived in that vicinity at that time.

One evening my father and I went to dinner with friends about two and a half miles distant from our home. As we left the house, my sister said, "They will be sure to urge you to stay all night, but don't fail to come home."

"All right," I answered, and we trudged off through the snow. After a pleasant evening we started home. It was a cold, still and moonless but starlit night. There had been a six-inch fall of snow and everything was covered with a mantle of white. Even the road was obliterated by its soft white covering and there was not a fence or a tree as a landmark. We started on over the trackless prairie in the direction of home, walking fast, for the cold was intense. We had only gone a short distance when my father was taken with severe cramps and was obliged to sit down. They became so painful that he told me to hasten home and send one of the boys back with a team for him. I flew over the prairie as fast as possible, never doubting, though the road was invisible, that I was going straight for home. But I finally became almost exhausted with running and it seemed as if I ought to be reaching home. I stopped and looked about me. There was nothing to be seen in any direction but the snow-covered prairie. I traveled on but began to be frightened. I knew that I had been traveling long enough to have reached home. I stopped again and considered. Coming to the conclusion that I must be going in a wrong direction and must, therefore, be lost, I remembered having been told that when one was lost on the prairie the thing to do was to find a buffalo trail and follow that; for it would always lead to the river and from the river one could get his bearings. I searched for a buffalo trail, found one and feverishly tried to follow it, which was not easy, for it was filled with snow. By this time I was thoroughly alarmed, fearing that my father would freeze or die of the cramps before I could get any one to the rescue. On and on I stumbled, following the trail.

Presently I heard men hallooing and guns being fired. This terrified me, for I knew that a gang of horse and cattle thieves were supposed to have their rendezvous in a canyon which perhaps I was nearing. Not stopping to realize that shouting and firing guns would be the last thing they would do, I turned and fled the other way. Then I saw a great bonfire with flames leaping to the sky. I stopped again with my heart in my mouth, wondering if it could be the fire of an Indian camp. But as I stood and watched it the light from the bonfire revealed to me the outlines of our own house. Taking a bee line for the fire, I was soon at home and great was my relief when I saw my father. He had waited a reasonable length of time and feeling a little better and fearing the cold, he had walked on home expecting all of the time to meet some one coming for him. When he entered the house my sister said, "Where is Laura? She promised to come home."

"Isn't she here?" asked my father excitedly.

"No."

"Well, then, she is lost," he said, and immediately sent for neighbors and organized and sent out search parties. They were "the horse thieves" and "Indians" I had heard, and it was their bonfire that lighted me safely home.

Little did I realize at the time that the experiences of this memorable winter were the buffetings that were molding me into shape for the life work before me. There was not one hard lesson that did not stand me in hand in after years.

One day there was a great tornado which swept over the country, leaving death and destruction in its trail. I happened to be at home alone at the time and just before the tornado came, a young man, not a professed Christian, called upon me. I had been talking to him about being a Christian. Suddenly the storm broke upon us in all its fury. The walls of the house rocked, and I ran to the window, terrified. The young man came and stood by my side and, seeing my perfect agony of fear, he said very quietly, "Why, Laura, where is your Christian faith?" I was humbled and rebuked, and as I lifted my heart in prayer to God, all sense of fear left me. The storm passed on and we were safe. But times innumerable during succeeding years when in peril on land or sea, the words, "Where is your Christian faith?" have come back to me with the comforting thought that in the heart of a true Christian there is no place for fear.

That winter I taught school again in the home district in the new sod school house. Early during the term diphtheria in its worst form visited our settlement. The first to die was a beautiful girl from my school. I closed school and went about from family to family, where need was greatest and helped nurse my pupils. There was only one family in the community where at least one member was not taken by death from that dread disease. That family was our own. My youngest brother, Robert, was so ill from it that the nearest doctor, who had come fifteen miles to see him, said there was no hope for his recovery, and that nothing more could be done. I would not give him up, though my mother begged me to "let him die in peace." I had done so much nursing that I knew all the remedies used, and I worked the whole night long using one after another of them and often lifting him in my arms and shaking him when the canker in his throat seemed to entirely stop his breathing. Just at dawn of that long night, large pieces of canker were loosened and removed, his breathing became easy and he was saved.

Death was so frequent in the neighborhood that one family buried two of their children in the same grave. One poor family buried five of their six children, all dying within a few days of one another. I nursed among them until smitten by the disease myself. The strain and the sympathy and long nights of nursing had told on me more than I realized and I was a long time regaining my strength.

Just before Christmas of the same winter my oldest brother, Charles, was stricken with typhoid fever. He and I had been almost inseparable. After his return from the Black Hills, he had been living alone. He was to have been married the following spring. He stopped on his way to the county seat on business one Wednesday morning and was feeling so miserable that I persuaded him to give up the trip and lie down. As he grew rapidly worse, we sent to Indianola, fifteen miles west, for a doctor. At that time the fastest method of travel was on horseback. The messenger returned late Saturday afternoon saying that the doctor (there was only one in town) could not leave his patients for so long a trip. After Wednesday night I did not leave my brother's bedside for anything except to swallow a mouthful of food or a cup of coffee when urged to do so. On Sunday morning we sent to Arapahoe, fifteen miles to the east of us, with another urgent call for a doctor. This time the doctor came, but my dear brother had passed on to the other shore before his arrival.

CHAPTER 3

COLLEGE AND CALL TO MISSION WORK

This was my first great sorrow. It brought heaven very near to me. It seemed to me for months that I could feel the dear presence constantly with me. Soon after this I went to the county seat, Beaver City, and took the examination for a first-grade certificate. I was successful and secured the first first-grade certificate ever issued in Furnas County. I was then offered the principalship of the Beaver City Schools, and taught there for a year. One afternoon while there, shortly after I had dismissed school, there was a rap at the door and upon opening it to my great surprise there stood before me my old school friend, Newell Dwight Hillis! It was Friday afternoon in the early autumn. He said, "Come and get into my buggy, and we will drive over to your home [seventeen miles] for the week-end and have a visit." This we did, and such a visit as we had! I learned that he was State Sunday School Missionary for the Congregational Church, and that I would probably see him frequently.

He was bubbling over with enthusiasm for his work and during the course of our drive he said to me, "Laura, what are you going to do with your life?" I told him of my longing to be a missionary but ended by saying that I supposed there was no use to think about that. "That would be splendid," he said. "Of course you are going to be a missionary. Nothing could be finer. Why do you say there is no use to think about it?" I told him that to be a missionary one must be educated. To be educated one must have money, and that on my small salary it was all I could do to support myself and help the home folks a little. "You have good health, don't you?" he asked.

"Perfect," I replied. "Then," he said, "you are going to be a missionary. There is nothing in the world to hinder." His enthusiasm was contagious. I have never in my life seen any one so capable of inspiring young people with high ideals as Newell Dwight Hillis when he was himself a young man. He was making his own way; he was going to have an education a good one. Anybody with good health could have an education if he tried hard enough. He told me of many of his own experiences and before we separated that week-end he had me inspired with a determination to go to school as soon as possible and to eventually enter foreign mission service. He encouraged me to get into touch with our Woman's Board and sent me a catalog of Doane College—the Congregational College of Crete, Nebraska.

From the time of that interview I never lost sight of my determination to be a missionary. All of my efforts were put forth with missions as my ultimate object.

The County Superintendent of Schools, E. N. Allen, lived in Arapahoe. He recommended me to the Board for the position of Principal of the Arapahoe Schools. I secured the position at an increased salary and boarded at his house. He was sent to the State Legislature as representative that year and urged me to try for the position to succeed him as County Superintendent, promising me his unqualified support. This, however, I refused to do, knowing better than any one else that my education was insufficient to self-respectingly hold such an office even if I could get it.

I had been saving my money and whenever I could spare enough to buy a calf I had been investing it in that way. These calves my father kept in his own herd and cared for without expense to me. It was the only way he could help me, and it was really a great help, for they rapidly grew in value.

After a year as Principal of the Arapahoe Schools, I decided to go to Doane College, believing that by boarding myself and practicing strictest economy, I could meet the expenses of one year in college and by this further education be better prepared for higher and more lucrative positions. A cousin who had been a classmate of mine at Franklin Academy in Illinois came West and went with me to Crete. We took a room and boarded ourselves, doing some close pinching financially.

College and Call to Mission Work

I think I may be pardoned for saying that we were in college for work and stood well both with the faculty and students.

My cousin had an uncle living on a farm some twenty miles distant. Once or twice during the late autumn he came in bringing us a huge basket of luscious tomatoes. For days and days these sliced raw with sugar, eaten with bread, formed almost our only food. To this day I never see raw sliced tomatoes without a mental picture of us sitting at our otherwise bare table, each with a large dish of tomatoes before her. We liked them, but just tomatoes and bread three times a day grew somewhat monotonous. Then imagine if you can—but you can't unless you have been a school girl away from home and boarding yourself—our transports of delight upon the arrival of a Thanksgiving box from Clara's sister in Illinois. That white fruit cake, jelly, nuts and fruit! Oh, they were glorious! We danced and capered around that box in a way absolutely unbecoming to a decorous would-be missionary. How little, insignificant things haunt one and cling to the memory in looking back over a life.

We took an active part in the religious life of the college, and it became known that I was preparing for foreign mission service. In this I was encouraged by President Perry and Professor Fairchilds, both of whom I loved devotedly. But I found the study of foreign languages hard—got better grades in everything else. I was speaking of this to the preceptress, Miss Merrill, one day when she said to me, "Do you not think, Miss Hardin, that you might take this fact as an indication that you are not called to foreign service?" This remark troubled me greatly, and filled me with doubt as to my calling. But it was God's method of impressing upon me the necessity of putting special effort in that branch of my education, for I afterwards led my class in Greek, though not without rising at four o'clock in the morning and putting my very best effort upon it.

About the time of my going to Doane College in 1880, the Nebraska Baptist Seminary was opened at the little town of Gibbon, with George W. Read as President. Three months before the close of the second semester at Doane, my people wrote me that there was smut on the corn stocks, which was causing disease and death among the cattle, so that I could not count on any more money from them that year. This news disturbed me greatly. There was no other source of income. Plainly I must leave college. It was too late to get a spring school. What should I do? Did it mean that I was to give up getting an education, that, in truth, I was not called to be a missionary when I had felt the call so strong? I went to class that morning with my mind and heart turbulent with such questions. At the close of the period I went back to our empty room and poured out my heart to God. I shall never forget that prayer, nor its answer. I told my Father of the straits I was in and begged him to make plain to me soon, very soon, so that it would be unmistakable whether or not He really wanted me to do foreign mission service. And if He *did* to open some way by which I might go on with my education. I prayed as I have seldom prayed before or since, and arose from my knees comforted. Less than a week later when I returned to my room late one afternoon, there was a letter for me. In the left-hand corner it bore these words: "Geo. W. Read, Pres. Nebr. Bapt. Sem., Gibbon, Nebr." Before opening it, I said, "There is the answer to my prayer." And it was true. With a wildly beating heart, for was not God Himself speaking to me, I read, as nearly as I can reproduce from memory, these words:

> Dear Miss Hardin,
> No doubt you have heard of the new Baptist School recently opened at this place. A few days ago my brother, Rev. I. W. Read, met on the train a friend of yours, Newell Dwight Hillis, who told him of you and said that you might be interested in this school. He spoke highly of your Christian character and said you were preparing for foreign mission service, but that you were about to be obliged to leave Doane College because of the condition of your finances.
> Now the fundamental object of this school is to develop Christian character; and its promoters desire more than anything else that the influences going out from the school be strongly Christian and reach to the ends of the earth.
> I read what Mr. Hillis said of you from my brother's letter to Rev. B. Bedell, a trustee of the School, who was present at the time, and he said at once "We must have that young lady here. I

will myself pay her tuition for the first semester, and once here, there will be no difficulty in her making her own way." He paid me the money on the spot, so your tuition for the first semester is already paid. I have also made arrangements for your board, which I feel sure will be perfectly satisfactory. So take this as the leading of the Lord and come to us as soon as possible. I will help you in every way I can, and I feel perfectly satisfied that you will be able to meet your financial problems once you are established in this school. Hoping to see you soon, I am very sincerely yours,

GEO. W. READ.

Could anybody doubt that being direct answer to my prayer? I did not. And a few weeks later I was in Gibbon. This was the spring of 1881. I entered the most advanced class, which would graduate in 1883. True to his promise, President Read did everything in his power to help me. As I had to begin some of my work six weeks behind my class, he advised me not to try to get work towards paying my board until this work was made up, especially as I was hoping at that time to go to China as a medical missionary and was taking a medical correspondence course from Dr. Anna K. Scott of Swatow, China, then in this country on furlough, and this took considerable of my time.

President Read went himself and arranged at a good comfortable place for my board and became personally responsible for meeting the bills. Then he planned my work with me and arranged to give me some teaching to do. He usually filled pulpits somewhere in the state on Sundays and was absent from his classes on Mondays. He excused me from some of my Monday recitations and allowed me to teach his classes that he was unable to meet, and also gave me some tutoring to do, so that I somehow managed to get through that semester.

Before returning the next year a dear old deacon in the church and trustee of the school who lived about two miles out in the country came to me and said that his son was not very bright along some lines he was studying and had a hard time to make his grades; and asked if I would be willing to come and live in their home and help his son and daughter a little evenings for my board. This I was delighted to do, and I shall never forget the kindness of Mr. and Mrs. Aschael Eddy and their children during that winter. But the weather was cold and the snow deep and the long, cold walk threw me out of most of the social life of the school.

At the beginning of this year there came a new student, Miss Minnie Buzzell, who afterwards went to China as a missionary, who became my classmate and friend. One day the lady with whom I boarded the first semester I was in the school sent for me. She said that she and her husband were going to be absent from their little home for several months—certainly to the end of the school year; that they did not want to rent their house furnished, neither did they want to pack their goods. She said if I would come and care for the house she would give me, my rent free and I could use such of her things as I needed for boarding myself and could ask any friend I chose to come and stay with me, suggesting Miss Buzzell, who was also preparing for mission work and who, like myself, was having a hard time to meet expenses. We were delighted with the prospect of having that cozy little home to ourselves, and promptly moved in. But I do not know what would have become of us that winter if God had not sent his angels, in human form, to minister unto us. For even there we must have fuel, food, and clothing.

We were told by a grocer, who was also a deacon in the church, to come and get anything we wanted. But neither of us believed in debt, and we would not go. Minnie's father came occasionally and brought us things from the farm. Nevertheless we learned what it was to go on short rations. People must have suspected how we were pinching, for we came home one day to find a fine lot of groceries and gingham enough for each of us a dress delivered at our door. We thought there had been a mistake but were told that instructions had been given to leave them there and say they were from a friend. There was nothing to do but take them and be thankful that God had given us such a friend.

One day I received through the mail an envelope containing a five-dollar bill, with nothing to indicate from whom it came. It bore the local post mark. Truly the ravens were feeding us! One evening our class came in for a surprise party. When they left we found a large package addressed to me. It was accompanied by a beautiful little note expressing their affection and asking me to allow them to do something practical to help me, that would remind me of their interest in the work I was preparing to do. The package contained a beautiful winter wrap. I have seldom ever had anything so touch my heart for the members of the class were nearly all poor and it meant real sacrifice on their part to give it, yet I doubt if they did many things while in school that gave them more genuine pleasure. No one will ever know with what deep joy I wore my beautiful wrap, for was it not absolute proof of the sincere confidence and love of my classmates? How wonderfully God was providing for me!

In March that year I had an opportunity to take the principalship of the Shelton Schools to finish out the year for a former teacher who had for some reason resigned. I took the position at what was at that time considered a good salary. My classmates sent me the lessons assigned every morning, and for three months I kept up my school work and taught at the same time. It meant hard work.

During the summer vacation of 1882 the school at Gibbon built a new ladies' dormitory. I was offered my room and board there in compensation for dining-room work. This I was glad to do for it made it possible for me to use some of the money I had earned for much needed clothing.

In a perfectly wonderful way God provided for me right through my school life. During my last term a former dearly loved teacher sent me forty-five dollars. She said she knew that I would need some money for graduating clothes and that I was to use this money for that purpose, and that when I got to the mission field and had a salary, I might put a like amount into my work as a contribution from her. This made it possible for me to accept her delicately offered help, and God alone knows what it meant to me. But much as I needed the money I think I can truthfully say that the evidence of my teacher's confidence and love meant far more to me than the forty-five dollars possibly could. And most of all I was impressed—almost awed—by God's wonderful provision for me, bringing me help in some unexpected way every time when there seemed positively no way out of my financial difficulties. Early in the spring before our graduation in June the Secretary of the Faculty called at our door and handed me a paper, while he smilingly congratulated me. No one could have been more surprised than I was when I read the note and learned that I was to be valedictorian of my class! It did not seem to me possible and to this day I truly feel that I did not deserve the honor. My classmates were lovely and seemed absolutely sincere in their congratulations, and the one most joyous over the honor having come to me was the one to whom I felt then as I feel now the honor should have gone—for without his help I could never have made the grades that took the valedictory. This person was Arthur Carson whom I afterwards married.

For some time before our graduation we were considerably concerned about our clothing for that great event. There were to be guests from all over the state, as well as from adjoining states, present at the graduating exercises of the first class to go out from our new Baptist School. What should we wear? We decided, after much thought and discussion, upon pretty blue wool dresses to be made by a local dressmaker. The question of gloves, shoes, etc., we talked over with a teacher recently from the East. It was just after small hoopskirts and "tilters" had come into vogue. We were told that it would never do to get up before the expected audience (it was thought Governor Garber would be there, as his son—or was it a nephew?—was a student in the school) without hoopskirts and white kid gloves. We wanted hoopskirts more than anything else in the world. *How we did want them!* But one of the young men in the class had made a remark about the "idiocy" of any girl who would wear a hoopskirt, that caused us, rather than disgust him, to decide to humiliate ourselves before the audience and appear "looking like string beans." Some way, I never knew how, the situation became known to the classmate who had made the remark. The evening before Commencement came and there was delivered to each of us a small package. As we cut the cords there leaped out before each of us, like a jumping jack, a pair of hoopskirts—a graduating gift from the young man! White kid gloves, which made us feel very self-conscious, were sent us the next morning by the lady teacher who had learned that we had none; and so again our wants, not needs this time, were miraculously supplied.

While our class was comparatively large when I entered it, only five of us completed the course. It was a remarkable class in its Christian interest and influence. One became a lawyer in Chicago, but because of the manifold temptations to shady practice, things not absolutely open and straight, he abandoned the law and entered educational work. He has been for many years, and so far as I know still is, an honored and loved deacon in the First Baptist Church, Chicago. One became a Congregational minister. He was known as a man who uncomplainingly tackled the hardest jobs and conquered them. One went as a missionary to China and on her return thrilled our churches, as few missionaries have been able to do, by her wonderful stirring appeals. One (Mr. Carson) spent twenty-two years of pioneer work in Burma, and the other (his wife) thirty-eight years of similar service.

From the time of my going to Gibbon I had been in correspondence with Mrs. A. M. Bacon, then Secretary of the Woman's Baptist Foreign Mission Society of the West. Her frequent letters were full of tender, loving advice, encouragement and inspiration. I feel that to her I owe much. I was always proud of being one of her "girls."

Shortly after my graduation on June 3rd, 1883, she invited me to come to Chicago for my examination, with a view to appointment for foreign service.

I went—as unsophisticated a country girl as one would care to meet. I had never been in a really large city and was absolutely unfamiliar with city life. I was taken to the home of Mrs. A. J. Howe, then President of the Woman's Baptist Foreign Mission Service, for entertainment. I was treated with every courtesy and got a vision of cultured life that up to that time the hard realities of my experiences had rendered impossible. That evening Professor Howe with his pleasing voice read aloud to us fine passages from Bickersteth's poems and commented upon them. I loved good literature and the evening was a delight to me. But when I went to my room I could not get away from the fact that I was to meet the Woman's Board the following morning. Would I fail to pass? How ignorant and self-conscious I felt. How humiliated and ashamed I would be if they refused to accept me. Yet how could they do otherwise? How little I really knew. I put in hours of torture when I ought to have been asleep. Supposing they should ask me to explain this, or this, or this, what would the answer be; how could I make my position clear? Over and over it all I went until my brain refused to act and finally I slept. Next morning with fear and trembling I met the ladies of the Board. Those present so far as I remember were Mrs. A. J. Howe, Mrs. A. M. Bacon, Mrs. C. F. Tolman, Mrs. J. A. Smith, Mrs. Everingham, Mrs. Wm. Haigh, Mrs. Brayman and Mrs. Randall. There were others whose names I do not recall.

They had a long list of carefully selected theological questions. To this day I remember, poor, ignorant, country girl that I was, how my heart sank as I faced that august body of city ladies and saw the long, neatly written list of questions. The grilling began and lasted for hours. How I ever lived through it I do not know, but I know that when the questioning closed, I felt a sense of shame and that I had failed ignominiously.

Friends in Dundee had invited me out there for the week-end. The ladies of the Board, after consulting together for some time after I left the room, called me back and asked me to return to Chicago on Monday morning and meet the Advisory Board after which the question of my appointment would be decided upon. The lady who was entertaining me had an engagement and could not well go with me down to the city. She asked me if I thought I could find my way alone down to our "Rooms" on Michigan Avenue. I had been there twice. If I was going to the other side of the world alone, I might as well begin to find my way here in Chicago; so I bravely told her that I was sure I could, though at the same time my heart sank and I thought of all sorts of stories I had heard of girls getting lost in great cities. I started out with a palpitating heart. I was told that if I knew the names of the Presidents in their order I would have no difficulty. These I had learned as a child and that knowledge encouraged me a little. But when I got on the street car and began to say them over, I could get to "Madison is the fourth, you know, the fifth one on the list, Monroe"—but who came after Monroe? Over and over it I went until all was hopeless confusion. To save my life I could only recall of the perfectly familiar rhyme, "Van Buren eighth upon the line and Harrison ranks number nine." "But who comes between?" I murmured and glancing out of the window I saw nothing that looked familiar, so left the car at the next stop. I wandered up and down but found no street name or anything to indicate where I was. I began to be very anxious. I must be at the station by a certain time or miss my train to Dundee. Supposing I should miss it? I had little more than enough money to pay my fare there and back, and I could never in the world go back to the kind lady who had entertained me. Just as I was beginning to be desperate (it had not occurred to me to ask information of a stranger, as I had been carefully taught never to engage in conversation with a stranger in a city), a huge policeman loomed up before me. Only a few times in my life have I been gladder to see anybody. I went up to him and said, "Will you kindly tell me where I am?"

With an amused smile he looked down at me and said, "My child, you're lost," and I was, but he soon put me right.

The trip to Dundee was filled with misgivings. Why had I ever supposed that I could pass a theological examination? What presumption! And yet, and yet, had not God made it very plain to me that He was leading me into Christian service? Had He not again and again answered prayer almost miraculously in opening closed ways before me? Still the ladies had looked very dubious and solemn, though sympathetic, when they asked me to return on Monday. The visit with Rev. A. W. Clark and his wife at Dundee cheered and comforted me greatly.

Monday morning found me again in Chicago. But if it had been such torture to face the Woman's Board, what would it be to meet the *men* and be quizzed by them? The chairman of the examining committee was Dr. Geo. Northrup. Others present whom I remember were Dr. Wm. Haigh, Dr. P. S. Henson, Dr. Geo. C. Lorimer, Dr. William Laurence, Dr. C. F. Tolman and Dr. Green of Evanston. All my life I have been proud to have had such a splendid body of men on my examining board. And all my life I have been grateful to dear Dr. Northrup for the tactful way with which he conducted my examination. He put me at my ease at once so that I was able to answer intelligently the few simple questions asked. They kept me less than half an hour, then asked me to go in where the ladies were waiting for me. Almost immediately one of their number followed me into the room and said: "It gives me great pleasure to announce that the Advisory Board heartily recommends the appointment of Miss Hardin for foreign mission service. Furthermore, it is especially requested that I say that the vote was *unanimous*." It seems, as I learned afterwards, that two of the ladies thought that my answers on the Office and Work of the Holy Spirit were not sufficiently clear, and recommended my remaining in this country for another year of study. The sense of relief when my appointment was confirmed was very great. I lifted my heart to God in a transport of joy and thanksgiving.

The ladies discussed the relative needs of the various fields. From the first, my eyes had been fixed on China, and my study had been mainly of that country. But the ladies said that the most urgent calls at that time came from Burma and asked if I would be willing to go there. I replied that I was perfectly willing to go where the need was greatest. Both Bassein and Tavoy, Burma, were pleading for single lady helpers for school work. Accordingly I was appointed for Burma, designation to be made later. Two days were spent in Chicago shopping for my outfit, for which a list of necessary articles was furnished me. It seemed to me that the list contained more articles than I could ever wear out. There were two print dresses, two white ones, two linen lawns, one black bunting and a summer silk. It was decided that the dark blue wool dress in which I had graduated and which I wore on the trip to Chicago (a really pretty and becoming dress) would be suitable and satisfactory for traveling.

It was not long after my return to Nebraska in June that I learned I had been designated to Bassein to take charge of their newly organized High School and that the date of my sailing was fixed for September 29th, the day after my twenty-fifth birthday.

The summer was spent in busy preparation for my long voyage. When the day came that I was to start my father was very ill; but it was my frail, delicate mother whom I never expected to see again, and I left with a heavy heart, though I tried to cheer them by saying that I would probably be back sooner than if I were being married and going to California to live, and they would not think of considering that in the light of a calamity. My father lived less than four years after I left and I never saw him again; but my mother lived to the ripe age of ninety-two and I had the joy of being with her on four different visits to the homeland. It was only on my last home-coming that I found her room empty of her dear presence, though filled with precious memories.

The Woman's Board was to be met in Chicago for final instructions, and a farewell meeting was given me by the Baptist students of the old University. I made a short address and was presented with a beautiful bouquet. The next day at the station I bade farewell to the last friends I expected to see for many years, and boarded the train for New York where I was to join a party of other missionaries.

Several ladies whom I met in Chicago and elsewhere told me how very glad they were that after reaching New York I would have the company the rest of the long journey of "dear Mrs. Jameson" who was to sail on the same ship. Long before I reached New York I thought of her as a friend beloved.

The last night before reaching New York I had no sleeper, but sat bolt upright all night long, preferring to have the money of the cost of a sleeper go into the Mission. That whole long night was a terrible nightmare; for there sat in the seat behind me an insane man whose son was taking him to an asylum. He constantly attempted to leap from the car window and kept me in a state of terror. This experience taught me better than to sit up nights to save mission money!

The relief was great when we arrived in the city and I saw the little red flag which was to introduce me to the messenger sent by Miss Newton, for many years chairman of the Hospitality Committee. I was taken to a dear old lady, a Mrs. Williams, who was much interested in missions, for entertainment. My own mother could not have been kinder. She gave me my breakfast, then put me to bed. After lunch she took me for a drive through Central Park and took me to other places of interest.

CHAPTER 4

FIRST VOYAGE TO BURMA

That night, September 28th, 1883, the night of my twenty-fifth birthday, farewell services were held for our party in the Berean Baptist Church, Dr. Edward Judson, pastor. Aside from the Jamesons I did not know who the other members of the party were to be. I did not much care. Had not Mrs. Marsh and others told me what a wonderful woman Mrs. Jameson was, and how I would love her? I would love *her* anyhow, and as for the rest it did not much matter. I could hardly wait to meet her and place myself in her hands; for I had been told that she would "mother" me, and I was tired, nervous and excited, and in great need of being mothered.

We met in the lecture room of the church—some one pointed her out to me. She was an austere woman and rather formidable in appearance, but I rushed up to her and introduced myself, rather effusively perhaps, for I was really delighted to see her. She shook hands with me very formally, coolly looked me over from head to foot as much as to say, "Well, who *are* you anyhow?"—and froze me to the marrow!

We got through the Farewell Services somehow, I scarcely know how. I met the other members of our party—Dr. and Mrs. Rose, Miss Aseneth Gage, and Miss Kathren Evans, all returning after furloughs—but the one thing that remains indelibly impressed upon my memory is *my disappointment in Mrs. Jameson*. Dr. Judson was most gracious and he and many members of his church arranged to meet us at the steamer next day. But how glad, *glad* I was to get back to my room! I threw myself on the bed, buried my face in the pillows and sobbed over and over again, "I don't like her! I don't like her! *I don't like her!*" meaning, of course, Mrs. Jameson. I can write this now because I have long since told her all about it; for there grew up between us, though she is twenty years my senior, one of the closest, sweetest and most precious friendships that I have ever known to exist between two women of any age—a friendship that has stood the test of almost forty years, which still exists and is growing more precious with added years, and which I confidently believe will continue to abide throughout eternity.

Perhaps the story of the long voyage can best be told by inserting here a letter written at the time and sent back to the *Nebraska Visitor*:

> ... We sailed on the beautiful Anchor line steamer, *Circassia*. I stood on the upper deck and watched the glistening spires and cupolas of New York slowly fade from view. When the last glimpse of my dear native land had disappeared beneath the horizon I felt that I had indeed separated from my dearest earthly friends. For just one moment an unutterable sense of loneliness stole over me. "And yet I will not forget thee." "In all places where I record My name I will come unto thee and I will bless thee." These words came to me in all their pathos and tender sweetness and laden with comfort and strength. I remained on deck until the approach of the much-dreaded foe, seasickness, compelled me to repair to my stateroom where I remained very ill almost the entire voyage across the Atlantic. Sometimes I almost thought to
>
> > "Sink beneath the waves with bubbling groan,
> > Without a grave, unknelled, uncoffined and unknown."
>
> But toward the end of the voyage, I was better. When the properly named "Emerald Isle" with its lovely green fields and pretty white cottages came in view I was able to be carried on deck to breathe the fresh, pure sea air and enjoy the scenery. I sat, almost all day, bundled up on a steamer chair and watched the great waves roll their beautiful, white, foamy crests up to the sun, never growing weary of their surging, ceaseless motion. The next day we passed under the very eaves of the Giant's Causeway

and peered among its cliffs and caves. It was a very beautiful and interesting sight, though the view from the steamer was unsatisfactory. We dropped anchor at Moville, Ireland, and allowed the passengers to go ashore. Anchor was cast at Greenoch that night, where we waited for the morning tide to bear us up the Clyde to Glasgow. About an hour before we reached the harbor the steamer *Tenasserim*, on which our passage to Rangoon was engaged, triumphantly passed us on her way out to sea. This left us no alternative but to go by rail from Glasgow to Liverpool and wait there for the boat. This was a journey of about eight hours' duration. The Scotland scenery was indescribably beautiful. The great heather-covered mountains, clear silvery streams flowing over solid rock or dancing and gurgling over pebbles, the beautiful skirts of woodland, green fields, thrifty little white stone villages nestling at the foot of mountains, and last, though not least, the barefooted, bare-armed, rosy-cheeked peasant girls, binding up the golden sheaves in the ripening oat fields, all served to make the day one of unsurpassed interest and pleasure to me.

We reached Liverpool on the evening of October 11th and took lodging until our steamer should sail, on the 15th. My impressions of Liverpool were not flattering, though the shop windows were the most artistically arranged and attractive of any I have seen. However, the city seemed very grimy and dingy and oppressive, and I was glad to leave it. The English cars, both street and railway, are very different from our American cars. The street-cars, or trams as they are called, have stairways running up the outside to seats on top. The last day of our stay in Liverpool we took seats on the top of one of these cars, and went to see the sights. We had a fine view of the city from our lofty position. The most interesting place we visited was Princess Park, which is nicely kept and is indeed beautiful. In the evening we went on board the *Tenasserim* and slowly sailed out of the mouth of the Mersey into the Irish Sea. The sea was very rough. The second night we had a hard gale. The settees were wrenched from the deck and the compass broken. The ship rolled and tossed like an egg shell for three or four days. Of the twenty passengers, all but one were seasick. For six days I was unable to be on deck; but I did not feel the want of sympathizing friends. On the evening of the 21st we passed in sight of the lights of Lisbon. Early the next morning we sailed past Cape St. Vincent—had a fine view. What we saw in Portugal and Spain seemed extremely barren and desolate. I arose at half-past three, the following morning, to view Gibraltar by moonlight. As I gazed at the great rock standing out in all its grandeur against the clear moonlit sky, I was filled with astonishment and awe. Is there not enough in nature everywhere to lead the mind to God if we will but behold it? On the opposite side of the strait could be seen the Rock of Centae, Africa. These two giant rocks are together called the "Pillars of Hercules."

The next place of interest was the island of Pantelleria, which we passed three days later. It is the island to which Italy banishes her criminals. We sailed near enough to get a good view of the city, which is built entirely of a light cream-colored stone. The island seemed fully desolate and lonely enough for the purpose for which it is used. The following day we cast anchor at Malta—the famous island where Paul was shipwrecked. Before we got near the shore our ship was literally surrounded with small boats, and peddlers with all sorts of things swarmed the deck. The loveliest laces I ever saw were exhibited on all sides, with the greatest persistency and determination to sell. Coral, silver and lava jewelry of quaint designs, canary birds, cunning, fluffy little lap dogs, boat loads of Maltese fruits—oranges, pomegranates, limes and prickly pears of enormous size, were urged upon us. It was a funny sight to see the boys dive for money dropped by the passengers into the sea. They never failed to bring up the coin dropped for them—either between the toes or the teeth—and with a grin and bow show it to the company. No sooner had we stepped on shore than we were surrounded on all sides by beggars, and we were harassed by them during the entire day—the halt, the lepers, the lame and the blind. We took gharries—rude wooden carriages—and went to visit places of interest. It is a strange, strange city. It is strongly fortified with stone walls said to be eighty feet high. The city is terraced and street after street is simply a flight of stairs hewn out of the solid rock which seems to comprise the entire island. The houses are all built of this light-colored stone. Not a single shade of anything else to relieve the glare. First we went to the great St. John's Cathedral. It was a grand sight. The quaintly carved walls and pillars, the beautifully frescoed ceilings, the marble slabs, covered with inscriptions, which formed the floor, the strangely dressed people coming in and dropping upon their knees before an altar covered with gold, were all objects of the most intense interest to me. From the cathedral we went to the governor's palace. First we went through a lovely garden, filled with tropical fruits and flowers. The council chamber was a place of special interest, the walls being hung with tapestry of most extraordinary character. It was presented by Louis XIV and cost 80,000 pounds sterling. It consists of scenes representing the different continents of the globe worked by hand in exquisitely shaded silk. We saw a coach said to have been owned by Napoleon the Great. We also saw no end of armor which our guide told us had been worn by "the great masters." Next we rode up to the bastion at the top of the terraced hill. I shall never forget the scene that met, my eyes as I looked out over city and harbor. The whole city looked as if it had been chiseled out of a huge block of stone. The sea was calm as a sleeping child, and the harbor was filled with ships from every nation of the globe, while the golden clouds in the sky were reflected from the quiet water's surface with no common splendor. Reluctantly I turned away and followed the guide into the catacombs. With a very solemn face he led the way into the tombs. Horrible sight! The mummies were not half so well preserved as I had supposed. The eyes were gone, the bones of the noses bare, and the grinning teeth exposed. They stood in niches hewn out of the stone, without anything to protect them from the dust of succeeding ages. Indeed they looked hideous and ghastly enough by the dim light of the wax taper carried by the guide. I was glad to get out of the horrid place into the fresh air again. Still I am glad I went, though I have no desire to repeat the visit at any future time. We left Malta that evening and four days later reached Port Said, Egypt, where we went on shore for a few hours. There was nothing of special interest to see except the surrounding desert and the strangely dressed people. There were Arabs in turbans and gowns, Turks in fezzes and bloomers and Egyptian women with covered faces, only the noses and ears visible and they (noses as well as ears) laden with jewels. We realized here that we were foreigners. My eyes had actually looked into Egypt! How far, far from home I was! "And yet will I not forget thee." "If I take the wings of the morning and dwell in the uttermost parts of the sea, even there shall thy hand lead me." Oh, the comfort of it!

It seemed a perfect Babel on shore, and we were glad to get back to the steamer, which, by the way, had come to seem quite like home to us. We had an unusually pleasant company and a captain unequaled in kindness.

In the evening we entered the Suez Canal. I was impressed with the great amount of labor it has cost. It is eighty-seven miles long and all the way through the desert. Scarcely a tree or a shrub is to be seen, except at the little stations where ships "tie up" for the night, and where the canal dredgers live. Around each of these houses are a few palm trees. We stopped at one of these little stations over night. The next morning we passed the road leading to Jerusalem and saw a caravan crossing into the desert, probably on their way to the Holy City. Arabs with camels and scrapers were at work along the banks of the canal. Two great baskets were hung across the camel's back; he knelt while they were being filled, and, at his master's bidding, arose and carried them away. Half-starved children, almost naked, would run out from the station and cry lustily to the passengers for "biscuits" and "backsheesh." Our steward provided us with ship biscuits which we flung to them in generous numbers. Just before entering the Bitter Lakes the captain invited me, with some others, to go up on the "lookout bridge" where we would have a good view of the little chateau which was built for Napoleon and Eugenia that they might witness the first vessels that passed through the canal. It is a beautiful place, but was occupied by soldiers in the late Egyptian war and is now in a state of ruin. That night we dropped anchor out in the lakes about one and a half miles from the shore at Ismalia, where the palace of the khedive of Egypt is located. The captain very kindly took some of us ashore in the ship's boat that we might see the town and palace by starlight, which was our only chance of seeing them at all. Scarcely had we stepped on the wharf before we were surrounded by young Arabs and their donkeys. We mounted the little donkeys, which were not larger than six-months-old colts at home, and with an Arab running after each one of us punching our donkeys with sharp sticks to keep them going, we proceeded on our way to the palace, a distance of perhaps two miles. We failed in our endeavors to gain admission into the palace on account of the lateness of the hour. After admiring the grounds and gathering some leaves to press and keep as mementoes we returned to our boat. Our row back to the steamer was most enchanting. It was a bright starlight night, the air had that mild softness known only to southern climes, and the friction of our boat on the phosphorescent water left behind us a shining track of glittering stars.

The next day we reached Suez and sent off mail on a tug. On the following day (November 3rd) we entered the Red Sea, which we found very smooth and quiet. On the morning of the seventh we passed the twelve small islands which the sailors call The Twelve Apostles. One stands off some distance from the others, which are quite close together. This one they call Judas Iscariot. In the afternoon we passed the Hanish group along the coast of which we saw five wrecked steamers. It is a very dangerous place for vessels to pass during the night time, or in the dreadful sand storms which are frequent there. In the evening of the same day we passed in full view of the city of Mocha, Arabia. November 10th we sailed out of the Gulf of Aden into the Arabian Sea, and passed the strange-looking Abdulkoori island, which some one suggested as looking as if it were packed in cotton on account of its base of white granite. In the afternoon we passed the "Two Brothers," the summits of which we could see far above the clouds. We saw several sharks near these islands—the first we had seen. Six days later we sailed past the beautiful little oriental island, Minikoi. It is literally covered with cocoanut palms, and is so low that they seem to be growing right up out of the water. We could see a lighthouse, in process of erection, and several fishermen's huts along the coast. There was nothing else of special interest until the 18th, our last Sabbath on board—when we passed Point de Gaul, Ceylon. This impressed me as being the most beautiful spot upon which my eyes had ever rested. The whole island is very beautiful and I do not wonder that the natives have a legend that the garden of Eden was situated upon it. The scenery is truly oriental—palm trees growing to the water's edge; graceful, feathery bamboos; lofty mountains towering above the clouds in the distance; and glistening white pagodas shining through the trees. As we neared its shores the first officer surreptitiously sprinkled cinnamon oil on the taffrail in order to hear the passengers exclaim about the "spicy breezes"—and verily he had his reward!

November 24th, early in the morning, the water changed from the beautiful blue to a muddy greenish color. This was evidence that we were entering the Rangoon River and in a very short time would be at the end of our long sea voyage, safely landed in Burma. It is twenty-five miles from Elephant Point, at the mouth of the river, up to Rangoon. Before we reached the wharf some of our Rangoon missionaries came out, in boats, to meet us and bid us "Welcome to Burma." Others from Rangoon and elsewhere were on the wharf to greet us. One or two stations sent a telegram, bidding us welcome. Safely landed on the wharf among all these kind friends I will leave us, reserving until another time my trip up the river to Bassein, my new home, my impression of Burma and its people. I will only add, for the sake of those who are personally interested in me, that I am well and very happy. With much love to the people of Nebraska, I am respectfully yours,

LAURA L. HARDIN.

CHAPTER 5

EARLY EXPERIENCES AS A MISSIONARY

Our captain had told me to provide myself with a pith hat or "topee" at Port Said and the missionaries, all going out after former service, also impressed me with that necessity. I got the hat, but it was very stiff, thick, ugly and unbecoming the brim lined with a ghastly shade of green. As we neared Rangoon I was eager to see the sights, so I finished my last packing early and dressed for going on shore. But that hat! Of course, I could not wear that thing with my natty black bunting so I put on a neat little straw turban, which went well with the dress, and sailed on deck. In my eagerness to get a good view of the strange looking people on shore and of the great Shwedagon pagoda, towering above the city and harbor, covered with gold from bottom to top and bedecked with precious gems sparkling and glittering in the sunlight, I ran from side to side of the steamer, as she varied her course, not being particular to keep under the double awning of canvas that was stretched above the deck to protect us from the vertical rays of the tropical sun.

The other missionaries, all familiar with the scenery, were still below attending to their last packing. Standing by the railing, my head with its thin covering exposed to the sun, and absolutely absorbed with the strange sights before me, I was suddenly brought to myself by some one seizing me by the shoulders and shoving me back under the canvas, at the same time exclaiming, "Why, Laura, don't you know better than that!" It was Dr. Rose, and it was a timely warning that he gave me, for I had already been sufficiently affected by the sun so that in all my thirty-eight years in the tropics I never fully recovered from the results of those few moments of careless exposure to its fierce rays.

Before our steamer docked, Mr. Phinney, the superintendent of our Mission Press, came out in a launch and came aboard. He had a package of home letters for me, and was the first to welcome us to Burma. All of the others of our party had friends, both missionary and native, to meet them.

I think I never felt so far away, so utterly homesick and alone as I did those first few moments at the end of that long, long voyage with no familiar face to greet me.

Then dear, beloved Mrs. Ingalls, that queen of women, came to the rescue. Panting and with her curls bobbing, she rushed up to me with a huge bouquet of red roses, saying as she presented them, "I just thought after I got started that all the others except you would have friends to meet them, and that would make you feel homesick, so I hustled back to the bazaar and got these roses for you. I had to hurry so I forgot my umbrella and left it in the bazaar, but I wanted you to know that somebody thought of you." How that little act of kindness touched my heart!

How strange were the sights and sounds when we stepped on that distant foreign shore! Everything seemed different, even the telegraph poles were square instead of round.

One little incident always comes back to me as I recall those "first impressions." Mr. Phinney called my attention to the rich and picturesque costume of an Indian gentleman with flowing white tunic over yellow satin trousers, the tunic surmounted by a gold-embroidered vest of purple velvet and the costume completed with jeweled red morocco sandals, turned up at the toes, and a gorgeous cap of purple velvet with rich gold and silver embroidery. Standing beside him was a coolie wearing no clothing except a very narrow loincloth. I was vexed with Mr. Phinney for calling my attention to an object I could not see without also seeing the practically nude figure by his side, and my face burned with indignation.

Poor little prude! Before we had reached the home of Mrs. Packer, where I was to be entertained, we had passed scores of groups of "nude figures" and they had already ceased to be a novelty.

After passing our medical examination, and getting through the customs, dear Mrs. Binney, with her snow-white curls, came down in her phaeton to meet me and take me to her niece's home, my place of entertainment, Dr. Packer's.

Mrs. Packer, aptly described as reminding one of the most exquisite piece of cut glass, her features so clear cut, her body so fragile, her conversation so sparkling, and her expression so pure and spiritual, received me with all the graciousness of the perfect lady that she was. The dinner was plain, but how good it tasted after the long weeks on the boat. It was hard, however, to throw off a feeling of discomfort with a solemn-faced, dark-skinned, white-turbaned servant standing behind my chair watching every mouthful of food and ready to grab my plate and rush off for something else the moment I laid down my fork.

Dinner over, my hostess soon ushered me into a very large room with the highest ceiling I had ever seen. Ceiling, walls, and furniture were of dark, unpainted teak, making the one small kerosene light look like a street lamp in a dense, London fog. In the middle of the room stood a bed easily wide enough for four people at least as wide as two ordinary double beds with a mosquito net fastened to the posts which had been extended about six feet for that purpose. The other furniture in the room consisted of a chair, the small teak table upon which the lamp sat, and a large teak almira (wardrobe), or jerusha as some one facetiously called it. Mrs. Packer showed me the bathroom, and looking about, said, "I think you will find everything necessary for your bath, which you will quite feel the need of after this hot day." She then told me not to be alarmed if I noticed little lizards on the wall. They were only geckos and quite harmless. Then there were touktoos (larger lizards) which frequently called out in the night and frightened people new to the country. They sometimes dropped from the ceiling, but the top of the mosquito net was made of muslin and would keep them from falling on the bed. After wishing me a restful night and, telling me not to get up for chota hazari (little breakfast) unless quite rested, she left me. I shall never forget my feelings as I took the lamp and looked around that big, bare room teak floor with no covering and saw the bright-eyed geckos peeking at me from places on the wall where I focused the light. I thought it the most desolate place I had ever been in in all my life. I thought of the possibility of a touktoo dropping from the ceiling before I got under the mosquito net, and decided to expedite my bath. I took the light, went into the bathroom and looked about. There was no bathtub! About a yard and a half square in the middle of the floor was latticed, and beside this square stood a very large stone jar of water. The top and bottom of the jar were about the size of a dinner plate; but it bulged at the sides so it held sufficient water for a good bath. But how did Mrs. Packer suppose that a girl of my size could ever get into that jar? I was nonplussed, and went to bed without a bath. Nevertheless there was a quart tin cup hanging by the jar of water and there was nothing to hinder my standing on the lattice, taking the cup and dashing the water over me, as I soon learned to do in taking one of the most refreshing baths yet known to human beings.

The following day I was taken around to call on the old missionaries. And what a galaxy of notables they were! All my life I have felt that it was an honor to know such souls as I met that morning the Braytons, Bennetts, Stevenses, Smiths, Vintons, Mrs. Binney and Dr. Gushing. We had to wait two or three days for our Bassein boat to sail, and I was invited to spend the remainder of my stay in Rangoon in the home of that prince among men, Dr. D. A. W. Smith, a worthy son of the author of our national anthem, "My Country, 'Tis of Thee," and at that time our mission treasurer. Mrs. Smith, a daughter of Dr. E. A. Stevens, was one of the most winsome women I have ever met and I always think of her as the most ideal Christian mother I have ever known. They had two small daughters in the home, Bessie and Emma (the latter now Mrs. H. I. Marshall of Insein, Burma). It was in this home that I received the greatest compliment of my life. The little girls and I became great friends; and before I left the mother overheard one of them say to the other, "If our mother should die, do you know who I want for my new mother?" "Oh, yes," said the other, clapping her hands, "Miss Hardin." "So do I! So do I!" And Mrs. Smith said in telling me of it that she thought they would be quite jubilant at any time over her demise!

The joy of the beautiful trip on a small river-steamer up the narrow, winding Bassein River to Bassein, was only tempered by a night of agony from ptomain poison when Mrs. Jameson—the unlovable (?)—worked over me the long night through and probably saved my life.

Upon our arrival in Bassein the night of the second day we were met by Mr. C. A. Nichols, now Dr. Nichols, and for more than forty years at the head of that wonderful work among the Bassein Karens, one of the most successful if not the most successful missions in the world. Miss Sarah Higby and Miss Isabel Watson, both of whom had gone out to Burma in the days of sailing vessels when they were six months en route and before the organization of the Woman's Society, also met me.

Miss Higby was then in charge of Pwo Karen work in Bassein and Miss Watson was to be my fellow-worker among Sgau Karens.

While in Rangoon, Miss Elizabeth Lawrence took me aside and said, "There are a few things I want to say to you in the hope of helping you over some hard places, for you are certainly coming to some hard places, and they will come from the source least expected. People are wont to think of missionaries as superhuman. But, although you will find among them the very finest people in the world, they are only human after all. It takes people of strong purpose and will power to break all home ties and come to the ends of the earth to submerge themselves and sacrifice their own lives in the effort to uplift a more needy people.

"Practically all of the missionaries certainly all of the best of them are people of very strong wills. When two very strong wills come together, nothing but the grace of God can prevent friction. Friction causes lack of harmony and great unhappiness. Besides, we are here to be examples to our people, and love and harmony should always prevail among our workers. Just pray for grace and try to see the truly good motives when things seem beyond human endurance." She did not mention a name and I tossed and tumbled in bed that night wondering what she could mean.

Thousands of times afterwards I had occasion to recall those words and bless her for them. Miss Watson was a tiny little woman weighing less than a hundred pounds. She was of Scotch descent and had a will of iron; but though blunt in speech and brusque in manner, never in my life have I known a woman of kinder heart or one more ready to sacrifice herself for others. However, things must go her way. So when we saw things from a different angle and failed to agree and I saw the unendurable approaching, I would grab her up in my big strong arms, take her across my knee and take off a slipper or call for a shingle. I invariably got her to laughing, after which she was ready to talk things over from my viewpoint, or after prayer over the matter together, consented to go with me to talk things over with Mr. and Mrs. Nichols and be guided by their judgment, which was usually excellent.

During the three years of my stay in Bassein we worked together in the greatest harmony. She stood up with me at my wedding, and I have rarely if ever seen a woman for whom I had higher esteem. But for Miss Lawrence's wise and timely warning, we might have been very unhappy together.

When we reached the mission compound on the night of my arrival it was after dusk; but the girls were all eager to see "the new mamma," so Miss Watson took me over to their building. Of course I could do nothing but smile at them as none of the girls at that time knew English. The answer to their first question was a disappointment. Did the new mamma sing and play? Was she musical, they eagerly asked. How my thoughts leaped back over the years to Aunt Nean's old piano and my brother George's ludicrously exaggerated characterization, for the amusement of neighbors and friends, of my efforts to sing and play. My cheeks burned as I had to confess to those music-worshiping people that I could do neither. After a short visit with the girls, with Miss Watson as interpreter, I was taken to my room, a room first occupied by Miss A. L. Stevens, who was the first woman sent out by the Society of the West and who was the last to say good-by and bid me Godspeed when I took the train at Chicago.

This room was not quite so large and was a little less gloomy, as the ceiling had been painted white, than the one in which I spent my first night in Rangoon. My bathroom was similar, but by this time I had learned to take a bath and enjoy it, in the real oriental fashion.

Older missionaries were convulsed when one said pyjamas, when she meant chota hazari, but how could one be expected to remember how to use all the Indian words she knew when she had been in the country less than a week?

Well, after chota hazari, and pyjamas too, for that matter, we went over to the great Kotha-byu Hall where teachers and students were congregated eagerly waiting to see the new "mamma" and to sing a hymn of welcome which had been prepared for the occasion. There were about three hundred boys and between forty and fifty girls, as I remember, and how they did sing!

Quite a number of the jungle Christians had come in to help in the welcoming of the new missionary. Most of these sat on the floor in the aisles, as they found the seats uncomfortable. Many of them had worn jackets, as a special mark of respect, but as the music went on and the heat of the day increased, one after another began hauling them off until I think nobody except students and teachers were clad above the waist. This was perfectly excusable, for the heat was intense and "nude figures" had already become the envy of my soul.

Nevertheless, dear old Christian hymns sung by that large company of strange people in quaint dress and undress but in the sweetest of voices, though an unfamiliar tongue, thrilled me and lifted my soul in rapture; and I thanked God for the opportunity of giving some of my life to their betterment.

After breakfast a teacher was brought to help me with the language a soft-voiced, sweet-faced girl armed with a spelling book.

I shall never forget that first day's experience. Po Po sat on the floor at my feet, went over the first line in the spelling book (I had learned the characters from Mrs. Rose on the voyage) then looked sweetly up into my face as much as to say, "Now you do that." But I didn't. I tried, but she shook her head in the negative and went over it again. Again I tried. Again she shook her head; she knew no English. Over and over it we went, she frowning a little but very patient. Finally exasperated, I said: "Well, what is the matter? I say it exactly as you do, yet you say it is not right. There is no use going on this way." She did not understand what I said, but we went to hunt Mamma Watson and find out what the trouble was. She laughed and soon had us straightened out. It was all in the tone. Each vowel sound had six tones and each variation of tone gave a different meaning. She illustrated by saying that one of my predecessors had thought she was telling one of the girls to bring her handkerchief which was lying on the bed. What she really did tell her was to bring her little husband who was lying on the bed. As the lady was of uncertain age and unmarried the girl was greatly amused. The difficulty was all in giving the wrong tone to the word wall.

For at least three hours every day I struggled with the language. I was to have charge of the newly organized high school, teach mathematics three hours a day and have the care of the sick boys. I soon learned to love the boys and girls devotedly and delighted in being among them.

When I had been studying the language for about six months, Miss Watson electrified me one evening by calling upon me to lead in prayer at the girls' prayer meeting. I struggled through it somehow, but the prayer was short. I was conscious all the time of having asked a Karen girl if it were true that a former "mamma" had been able to pray in Karen after studying the language only three months. She replied, "Yes, she did. I hope God understood her. We Karens couldn't."

I was slow at the language. My unmusical ear was not quick to distinguish the variation in tones. It was a full year before I dared undertake teaching a Sunday School class; and even then I had to make careful preparation and then go over it all thoroughly with my language teacher before appearing before my class.

During this season of language study, however, I had the opportunity of teaching in an Anglo-Indian Sunday School, conducted by the Jamesons in the Burman Mission Compound. This Sunday School was in session from seven to eight o'clock in the morning. I greatly enjoyed the early Sunday morning walk, and being able to teach in my own tongue. One or two from that Sunday School class went to England to study and afterward became quite prominent men among their own people, notwithstanding the fact that when I asked one of them to tell me about Simon the Sorcerer, he replied, "Why, he and Paul tried to play tricks on a girl!"

Before the long, hot-season vacation came the annual Government examination of the schools. As the time drew near, it was interesting and sometimes amusing to note at the prayer meetings how earnestly boys and girls prayed that they might pass. We felt that if they applied themselves as earnestly to their books that there would be no failures, and really there were few.

The girls trembled with subdued excitement the morning the Inspector, an Englishman, arrived. He kept them for two whole hours in that state of agony before beginning his work. But in the main although too frightened and shy to speak, the girls did very creditably, especially in music and needlework. They were very winsome with their sweet, shy ways and one could not fail to be charmed by their clear birdlike voices, when they sang. Their needlework was exquisite.

In examining a class of boys in Geography, the Inspector asked a bright boy to give proofs that the earth is round, a fact that Burmans discredit. The boy glibly gave the well-known proofs. "Do you believe that?" asked the Inspector. "No, sir!" promptly replied the boy.

There was a large jungle school a few miles out from town which also had to be inspected and Mr. Nichols invited me to take my first jungle trip in company with himself and the Inspector. I was particularly anxious to go, as there was to be a Karen wedding solemnized by Mr. Nichols while there.

We started before sunrise, riding small Burman ponies through narrow, winding jungle paths, the boughs, dew-laden, often brushing our faces. We found the ride exhilarating and ourselves, upon our arrival, with ravenous appetites.

This was well, for watching the women cook our breakfast over an open fire by the side of the house, in vessels encrusted on the outside by the accumulation of ages, one found it natural to wonder as to the condition of the inside when our food was put in. I felt while the cooking was going on that I could not eat food that came out of those vessels, but I did and enjoyed it. The rice was as white as snow and deliriously cooked. I saw them boiling eggs and my spirits rose. Here would be something that I could eat without qualms. But alas! They carefully removed the shells with hands none too clean and served the eggs, spotted with fingermarks, in a dish the outside of which had not been washed for a generation.

They went out and milked the buffaloes in order to furnish us with fresh milk. This the Inspector enjoyed and recommended; but the cocoanut dipper had been used too often to be attractive. Besides, the milk looked bluer than the heart of an iris and neither Mr. Nichols nor I got up courage to sample it.

That was forty years ago. There are people in that village now who could serve as clean and dainty a meal as one could wish.

After breakfast came the examinations. The Inspector put a native man in charge of the work, and being quite an artist proceeded to amuse himself and us by drawing pictures of interesting sights presented. One was of a young mother, her dress beginning at the point of her hips (even a trifle lower than those worn by the American "flapper" in 1922), smoking a huge cigar and carrying a child on her hip, who was clad in a pair of bright-colored yarn earrings. This was a Burman Buddhist mother and child, not a Madonna.

Examinations over, then came the wedding. When everything was ready the bride, being shy, ran up stairs and no amount of persuasion would induce her to come down. Her friends giggled and plead with her, but to no purpose. Finally several of them literally dragged her down the stairs and to the place in the yard where the ceremony was to be performed. She promptly turned her back on the preacher. Her friends turned her around and held her. The preacher took hold of her hand to place it in that of the groom. She savagely jerked it away and put it behind her. Finally, however, the groom got hold of it. Again she jerked it away, but after a struggle he got it again and the ceremony was completed. The bride immediately rushed up stairs again and the groom trudged off over the rice fields to his home without her. However, he no doubt returned after we left and "ate rice" with her in the presence of the village elders which would be a satisfactory conclusion of ceremonies to both parties concerned.

About sunset we rode back to the mission after a delightfully interesting day.

CHAPTER 6

VACATION DAYS AND MISSIONARY TRIALS

As my first hot-season vacation approached, Mr. and Mrs. Nichols planned to go to Chaungtha, a small island off the coast in the Bay of Bengal, where they owned the only house on the island. They invited me to take my language teacher and accompany them and Miss Watson to that delightful spot where there were always fresh sea breezes, and where sea bathing was ideal.

We had to ride elephants over the mountains to the coast. That first day's experience in elephant riding is long to be remembered. A mother elephant that had a baby and was considered exceptionally gentle was brought for us three women and little Harry Nichols and his nurse.

Quilts and cushions were arranged in the huge howdah, which was securely strapped on the great beast's back; then the immense, ponderous creature got down on her knees for us to mount. This we did by stepping on her knee, reaching a hand to the driver—a Karen man who sat on her head—and climbing. With the driver's assistance, we managed to reach her "ridgepole" in safety and then, gingerly balancing ourselves, make our way back to the howdah and get in.

The sensation when she started off, with her long lumbering steps, made us feel that we would surely go over her head and was worse than seasickness. But we soon became accustomed to it and delighted ourselves with watching our wonderful animal.

She was guided by the driver punching her behind the ears with his bare toes. But she needed little guiding. Never in my life have I seen such human intelligence displayed by a dumb animal. She watched every small tree or branch along the narrow path that was likely to strike the occupants of her howdah, and either broke it off with her trunk or crushed it to the earth with her powerful foot. Furthermore, she was as solicitous for her baby as any human mother over her child. She carefully kept it in the path before her and whenever it would turn off into the jungle she would reach out and tenderly draw it back. When we came to short, steep places in the path, she would either boost it along with her head or lift it gently over the step too steep for the short legs.

When we reached the coast Mr. Nichols procured a small row boat and with his comforting admonition to part our hair exactly in the middle and hold our breaths, we set out for the island which we reached in safety and found a most charming spot.

The following day we went over to the mainland to look about. Some friendly people met us and, not often seeing white people in their vicinity, wanted to pay us some attention. They presented us with some green cocoanuts the water of which we drank and found most refreshing after our hot walk on the beach. Then a woman smilingly invited us to come into her house out of the fierce sun and rest. We felt flattered and gladly accepted her invitation. After chatting with her for some time and in accordance with oriental etiquette, asking about the members of her family, she replied that her husband was very ill. When we asked if he were away from home, "Oh, no," she replied, "he is here," pointing to a heap at the end of the veranda, on which we sat, on bamboo mats on the floor. Mr. Nichols politely got up and went over to speak to him. The poor man was just one writhing mass of smallpox. Since we did not have any of the medicine of which a Burman doctor once told my husband, we did not make our stay longer than necessitated by common politeness.

The doctor referred to was living in a large Burman village. My husband visited him, and while they were chatting a man rushed in and asked for medicine, saying he feared his wife was dying. The doctor without saying a word leisurely arose, took a large package from the thatch overhead, measured out a huge dose and gave it to the man, without asking a question, and sat down again to resume the conversation. Being somewhat curious, my husband asked what was the malady of the woman for whom he had just prescribed. "I don't know," the doctor replied. "You don't know?" said my husband in astonishment. "Then how can you prescribe for her without seeing her?"

"Well, you see it is like this," he said. "I have studied all of the ninety-six diseases and I have found a cure for every one of them. I mix the medicines, so no matter what the disease is, the patient gets the medicine that is good for him. So you see," he said cheerfully, "it is not necessary for me to see my patients."

"And do they all get well?" asked my husband.

"Oh, no," he confessed. "Most of them die."

After spending a delightful three weeks at Chaungtha we returned to Bassein. When Mrs. Carpenter returned to America, she packed her household linen in a camphor-wood chest and left it in Miss Watson's care, intending at that time to return to Burma after a short furlough. Having more of this world's goods than most missionaries, she had unusually beautiful table linen and a large supply of it. Miss Watson's last care before leaving for Chaungtha had been to fill little chatties (bowls) with "earth oil" (crude kerosene) and set the legs of the stand on which the chest sat in them to prevent possible depredations from white ants, though it was supposed camphor wood was immune. The chest was in a porch inclosed with lattice, covered with creepers.

The next morning after our arrival from Chaungtha Miss Watson called out in a most distressed voice, "Miss Hardin! Miss Hardin! Do come here!" I went to discover that the leaves had blown in and settled on the earth oil, which is death to white ants, and the ubiquitous little pests had seized their opportunity, built their little secret trail over the leaves and entered the precious chest. Upon opening it only a mass of dust and a few hems were to be seen. I do not think there were two square inches of unchewed linen in the whole great chest. Poor Miss Watson, always so faithful to any trust, how terribly she felt!

Soon after our return from vacation the rainy season began, and so did the measles. Miss Watson had charge of the sick girls, I of the sick boys. The boys were scattered in fifteen different houses—one dormitory and fourteen cottages, as I remember. All of these buildings were up from the ground and all the boys slept on mats spread on the floor. There were thirty-five boys down with measles at one time, some in each house. This involved going up fifteen flights of steps, not very long ones, and kneeling down on the floor to take temperatures and give medicine at least thirty-five times every time the rounds were made, which was not many times a day for the days were not long enough. The greatest trouble I had was with diet. Friends would come from their jungle homes to see the sick boys and would persist in giving them, on the sly, raw cucumbers, ngapi (putrid fish), dried fish, chillies, or any other delicacies they happened to crave that were obtainable. I felt well repaid for all my hard experience and lame knees, for not one boy who remained in my care died, though several who were taken home did. Measles, a disease which will not brook dampness and exposure, is almost as greatly feared by the Karens as cholera, and when in their own homes almost as liable to be fatal.

Shortly before my second hot season in the country, there arose a disturbance among our people over a matter of discipline. Mr. Nichols was severely criticized by some native teachers who had studied in America and who felt that they should be put on an equal basis and an equal salary with American missionaries, though their method of living required less than a fourth as much expense.

They used this matter of discipline to stir up discontent among the patrons of the school. Finally some of the leaders came and suggested that the management of this most important mission school in Burma be turned over to the Karens themselves.

When Mr. Nichols told me about it, "That is exactly what I think we ought to do," I said. "What, do you think they can manage this big school themselves?" he exclaimed. "Not for a minute," I said. "But they think they can; and they will never be satisfied until they have had the trial. Besides if they can do it, they ought to do it and thus relieve you for evangelistic work and give you more time for the superintendency of the Press. If they cannot manage it, they have got to learn it for themselves by actual trial," I replied. After thinking a little, he said, "I believe you are right," and we went and talked the matter over with Mrs. Nichols and Miss Watson and very soon, after earnest prayer, decided to turn the school over immediately.

The Karens had built the good teak buildings with their own money and, barring the salaries of the missionaries, the school was supported entirely by the Karens themselves; so they had a right to run it if they wished and could. Mr. Nichols called the trustees and leading men together and told them of our decision. That they might feel perfectly free to try out their own plans and not feel that they were being watched and criticized by the missionaries, it was thought best for Miss Watson and me to go elsewhere. Mr. Nichols would look after the Press and Book Bindery but spend most of his time traveling among the villages preaching the Gospel.

This was shortly before the last Burmese war and the taking of Upper Burma, and the country was in a state of suppressed excitement and agitation. Bands of dacoits were rising up all over the country and committing all kinds of depredations. Mr. W. F. Thomas of Henzada had become greatly interested in the Chins of Arracan who had never had any mission work done among them. He wanted to make a tour among them and learn more of their numbers, accessibility and needs. He therefore invited me to come to Henzada and stay with his wife during his absence with a view to working among the Chin people should he succeed in inducing the Board to open up work among them.

Dacoit bands were becoming more and more bold, spreading terror all over the country. The day I left Bassein for Henzada the Deputy Commissioner (British) who had been out after them was brought in, a corpse. It was vacation time and Mrs. Thomas and I stayed alone in the large Karen Mission House.

The Superintendent of Police told us that dacoits had threatened to burn the town and advised us not to stay there alone nights. Accordingly we went every night to the Burman Mission House, occupied by the Hascalls, to sleep. After going over one night after dark a Karen came in great excitement showing us rags soaked in kerosene which he had found placed under our house and other buildings on the Karen compound and which had without doubt been placed there with the intention of burning the buildings. Mr. Hascall hurried with the news to the District Superintendent of Police. He immediately ordered us all into the courthouse, which he had strongly guarded, and ordered another guard to patrol the mission property all night. Rumors had gone abroad that the town was to be looted and burned that night and the courthouse was already full of terrified natives. Mrs. Hascall and

Mrs. Thomas both being in delicate health, we finally got the reluctant consent of the District Superintendent of Police to remain in the Mission House. But he came personally several times before morning to make sure that we were safe.

Shortly after daybreak we heard a peculiar sound like "the sound of a going in the tops of the mulberry trees." The dhoby (washerman) came running in and threw his great bundle of clothing from his head to the middle of the floor. Some of the clothes were washed and ironed, some were soaking wet, and some were still unwashed. "They are burning the town! They are burning the town!" he screamed as he ran toward the courthouse for protection. We rushed to the window. Sure enough, we could see smoke! People were rushing here and there in wildest panic and terror. Fire had been started in the outskirts of town, but the District Superintendent of Police, a fine officer, was on his job and soon had things quieted. But the excitement and anxiety of that season, during which time a little boy was born into the Hascall home, and shortly afterwards another to the Thomases, were experiences long to be remembered.

If my memory serves me right, the Karens ran the school for three months. Then came the long vacation. They were unable to manage the finances or to keep things up to anything like their former standard. They had their lesson, and discovered that they were not yet ready to assume large responsibilities.

They came back and begged us to resume the responsibility of the school, promising to work with us in harmony in the future. This we cheerfully did. That was thirty-nine years ago. Mr. Nichols has been with them ever since and the world-renowned achievements of that splendid Mission is proof of his wise leadership and the earnest and consecrated efforts of that wonderful people.

CHAPTER 7

SHWE PO AND AUNG BWIN

On my return to Bassein there came to me one morning a bright-faced, dirty, ragged young urchin, saying that he was an orphan, that he wanted to go to our Mission school and had come to see if I would help him get work to pay his expenses. After making some inquiries I told him to come and I would give him work out of school hours.

He made fine progress and after leaving Bassein I continued to help him for a time. He finished his High School course and I heard he had secured a position under the Government. After that I lost track of him. To finish his story here, and at the same time reveal one of the most precious compensations of a missionary's life, let me turn aside from the regular chronological order of my story. Many years after, when coming down the Chin Hills on my way home on furlough, shortly before we were to start down the mountains we heard that a British general, with his retinue, was on his way up the Hills on inspection duty. As the tiny bungalows at the end of each day's march on the Government Road were only accessible to us by the kind courtesy of the Government, having been built for the use of officials and furnished with cots, chairs and tables, and as these bungalows were too small to accommodate both the general's company and mine, we decided in conversation with Mr. Fischer, Assistant Superintendent of the Chin Hills, to take a much less frequented trail on which two of the bungalows had been destroyed, and which would involve an extra day's travel in a rowboat. The Assistant Superintendent most kindly offered to send men ahead to build grass huts where bungalows had been destroyed so we would have a safe place in which to sleep each night. This he did. Dr. Woodin, new to the country and unfamiliar with the language, was to accompany me. Neither of us had ever traveled the road before, so we started out on our long trail veritable babes in the woods. We sent boys ahead with a cooked dinner, telling them to stop at the first village and await our arrival. But the village happened to be off the main trail and we passed it by, riding on for miles without coming to any village. As it began to grow dark and as we were surrounded on all sides by dense jungles, we decided to retrace our steps. After riding for miles we finally saw a light and soon heard voices. The boys, after waiting till night-fall, suspected what had happened and were out on our trail. We went back to the village, had our dinner and remained over night. The next few days were passed pleasantly enough. The little grass huts that had been built for us looked like dolls' houses. They were fresh and clean, with a partition through the middle, and the men had put a pile of grass on one side in each room for a bed, and had driven posts in the ground and made us a table about eighteen inches square, in front of the house. It was like living in Fairy Land! But when we reached the foot of the mountains, our bungalow was in the midst of a great, sizzling, dusty paddy (rice) plain and was surrounded by herds of water buffaloes.

Dr. Woodin made an arrangement with a boatman to take us all the way to Kalemyo in order to save unloading and reloading the goods, though it was not customary for one set of boatmen to go farther than one day's trip, which would be to Indin. Not knowing whether or not I would ever return to Burma, I was taking home some of my husband's most treasured books, curios, household linen, etc. Furthermore, I had some of the beautiful hand-woven silk for my prospective daughter-in-law's trousseau, to say nothing of a box of dainty garments which friends had sent me from America in order that I need not appear in last century's costumes upon arrival in civilization. Altogether there were several trunks and boxes.

We got a boat large enough to hold them all and started gayly down the river. About the middle of the forenoon I noticed water slopping about my feet. I told Dr. Woodin and we both began to bail. The water gained on us, however, and we were obliged to land. We had three boatmen. They went cheerfully to work, calking the cracks in the boat, while our cook gathered sticks, made a fire on a sand bar and cooked our breakfast. Breakfast over and the boat reloaded, we journeyed on, but we had only traveled an hour or two when I saw a stream of water the size of my little finger spurting up at my feet like the water in a drinking fountain. Again we had to land and unload, and this time turn the boat over to do the calking. We were long delayed and instead of reaching Indin in the early evening, it was about nine o'clock at night when we got there. The boatmen being unfamiliar with the river at that place landed us on the opposite side from the bungalow where we expected to spend the night. As we wanted a safer boat for the remainder of the trip, and as the thugyi or headman to whom we must apply lived on the side where we had landed, we hunted up his house, got him out of bed and asked him to furnish us with a boat to take us across the river that night to the bungalow and on to Kalemyo the following day. He was very affable, gave us seats and told us just to wait and he would have a boat ready for us very soon. We waited long for his return. Finally he came, saying our boat was ready. We went down a long steep bank and found—the same old leaky boat in which we had come! My trunks and boxes were sitting in several inches of water! "Why, this is the same boat," we said. "Yes," said the thugyi. "I could not get my men together to get you another boat to-night, but this will get you across the river all right and I will send you a good one in the morning." There was nothing else for it. They had brought the boat farther down the stream than where we had landed and it stood in shallow water some distance from the shore. We had to take off our shoes and stockings and wade out to it. I had just dressed my feet again and was starting to enter the "paung" or part covered to protect one from the sun, when Dr. Woodin said, "Why do you go back in there? Why not stay out here where it is cool." I returned and sat on the end of a box by his side. If I had not done so I would probably have been drowned, for only a few moments later our boat struck a rock and with a great crash turned over, throwing us and all its contents into the water. It was by almost superhuman effort that the Doctor kept the boat from closing down over us, as it certainly would have over me, had I been inside. As he kicked the boat away, with wonderful presence of mind, he threw his hand under my head to keep me from sinking as we were thrown backwards into the water. Our only light was a kerosene lantern and this of course went out with the capsizing of the boat. We floundered about in the water in the dark until somehow the Doctor succeeded in getting me ashore. Then the work of saving the goods began. The boatmen worked like beavers, and it was not long until most of the things were rescued. I saw the suitcase in which I had some precious translations on which I had worked for months, and the Doctor's big pith hat sail by and I waded out and saved the suitcase. So far as I know to the contrary, the hat is "going on forever." The Doctor had to travel nights on his return, not because his "deeds were evil," but because he had no hat to protect him from the fierce and dangerous rays of the sun. The water was cold; it was late at night; we were on the wrong side of the river; our boat was a wreck, our clothes were soaking wet and we had had no dinner. Our food was in the bottom of the stream. What were we to do? One of the boatmen knew of a small empty bamboo house where Englishmen stopped when they came that way. We told them to take the bed bundles and, leaving the other things piled together, lead the way to the empty house. With our shoes full of cold water and our clothes dripping, we dragged ourselves up a steep bank of pure sand which clung to our clothing and weighted our feet. The road to that bamboo house seemed endless, though in reality the distance was probably less than a mile and a half. Our lantern had gone down with the boat and our matches were all wet. We had to send a man to get people out of bed to borrow matches before we could get a light. The house had one small room and a tiny bath room—no furniture. Dr. Woodin generously allotted the larger room to me, taking the bathroom, in which he could not straighten out full length, for himself. We opened our bed bundles, which were wrapped in supposedly water-proof canvas, hoping to find something dry for we were shivering with cold. "Are any of your things dry?" asked the Doctor. "Not a blessed thing! Even the pillow in the middle of the bundle is soaked," I answered with despair in my voice. "Never mind. I have a bath towel and a suit of pyjamas that are only damp a little. You may take your choice," cheerfully offered the Doctor. "I'll take the bath towel," I said. "Well, give yourself a very thorough rub with it until you feel warm," he said, "for I shall be surprised if we do not have a fine case or two of pneumonia here by morning." I did as he recommended, then wrung the water out of my clothes and the wet bedding, spread the quilts on the floor and with a raincoat for covering, went supperless to bed. Long before daylight I got up, dressed in the raincoat, pulled some bark off the rail fence, made a fire and piece by piece dried my clothes and put them on. They were streaked and blackened with smoke, but I felt like a Million Dollars when I got them on after the experiences of that awful night. When clothed and in my right mind once more, I sent a man to get some rice. This we cooked and ate and then proceeded to make preparations to continue our journey, for we could lose no time or I would miss my boat to Rangoon. When we went back to the river bank we found that the trunks and boxes had been submerged so many times in the rescuing that the contents were soaked. We also found it impossible to get a boat big enough to take all the goods. We had no time to open boxes and dry the contents. We simply had to go, taking such things as we could and leaving the others sitting on the bank to soak. I did not see them again until ten days later. When I heard the swish-swash of water in the trunks we had with us and opened them only to find my Mandalay silk and other treasures soaked, streaked and stained, I was utterly heartsick. How could I go on to America with every article of finery ruined? I took my box of millinery and pitched it overboard. My wedding fan followed it; then a treasured fan of great beauty given to me by the niece of a former Premier of Belgium went to keep them company. Treasure after treasure followed suit.

It was a dilapidated-looking missionary, and a decidedly disheartened and "blue" one, that set foot on the bank at Kalewa the second evening after the wreck. But as we climbed the bank there came towards us a fine-looking native gentleman, handsomely dressed in the picturesque Burmese costume and carrying a package of letters in his hand. "Why, Mamma Carson," he said, "don't you know me? I was your boy in Bassein twenty-five years ago. I heard you were coming and I got your mail and came down to meet you. Let me know your wishes and I will do anything I can for you." When asked how he came to be there he said, "Oh, I am myook [mayor] of Kalewa now." He paid our boatmen and coolies, sent fresh bread, milk, fish, cocoanuts, and many other things, to the bungalow for our comfort, and when the steamer came in he saw my things on board and insisted on paying my steamer fare to Monywa whence I would go by rail. Had I been his own mother he could not have seemed more glad to see me, nor treated me with greater kindness. *My little ragged orphan boy*, whom I had helped so long ago! God bless him! What a fine man he was.

Two days later I reached Monywa and before we docked a Karen man with beaming face came on board saying, "Mamma Carson, I am so glad to see you. I heard you would be on this steamer and I came to meet you. I used to be one of your High School boys twenty-five years ago. I am now Havildar [captain] of the Military Police stationed here."

That night I was entertained in the English Wesleyan Mission. Mr. Winston said to me—"That Karen Havildar of yours who is here is a wonderful man. I don't know how we would get along without him. He leads our choir [there is no Baptist mission at Monywa]; he teaches in our Sunday School; he is always at prayer meeting and helps in every possible way in our Christian work. Then that Baptist Christian Burman, S. D. O. [Sub-Divisional Officer] who has headquarters here—he is one of the choicest men I have ever seen. If your whole Baptist mission had done nothing more than to develop such a character, it would be well worth all it has cost. Whenever he is here on the Sabbath he goes about and gathers up a lot of the most influential men in the place—because of his high position any of them are proud to be seen in his company—and brings them to church. Frequently I ask him to preach. He never refuses, and he gives them some of the finest talks to which I have ever listened. I only wish I could do half as well myself. He is one of the finest characters I have ever known—white or black."

My train left at four o'clock the next morning and when I reached the station there was that splendid Burman Christian official up and out at that time in the morning to see me off and wish me Godspeed!

As I traveled down country and had time to think things over I said to myself with an overflowing heart, "What do I care for ruined finery—the spoiling of my goods! *Things* do not matter. It is *human lives* that count! What splendid compensation for all the trials of past years to have the evidence that God has given me during these past three days to carry home with me evidence that our Christians are making good. Evidence that God has so honored *me* as to give me some little part in helping to uplift a nation."

Before I came home the last time—1920—I received a beautiful letter from my orphan boy saying he had heard that I was going home to retire; that he had tried to get leave from the Government to come to Rangoon to see me off but had failed. He wanted to thank me for what I had done to help him to make something of his life, etc., etc. He was then Station Magistrate and Treasury Officer in the seaport city of Maulmain; a man looked up to and loved by British officials and natives, heathen and Christian alike, because of his splendid sterling Christian character. He has been three times honored by the British Government and has a right to write six letters after his name.

CHAPTER 8

MARRIAGE AND FIRST MISSION TO CHINS

But to take up the thread of my story—about the time of my return to Bassein in the spring of 1886 Rev. Arthur E. Carson was appointed by our Board for service in Burma to open up work among the Chins—a people who had never had a missionary of any denomination, but among whom some work had been done by Rev. E. O. Stevens, the elder Mrs. Thomas and Rev. and Mrs. W. F. Thomas.

Mr. Carson, to whom I was engaged before leaving America, but who remained behind to pursue his theological studies, was to sail in September. We were to be married immediately upon his arrival. While in Henzada with the Thomases I had engaged a native man to weave by hand the material for my wedding gown. It was white silk woven on a hand loom on the ground under a bamboo hut. I furnished cloth to keep it covered and went down frequently to make sure it was not being soiled. That spring Dr. and Mrs. Nichols went home on furlough and I sent the silk to New York by Mrs. Nichols to be made up and sent back by Mr. Carson. It was a beautiful dress.

During the absence of Mr. and Mrs. Nichols, Miss Watson and I carried on alone. Mr. and Mrs. Price were coming with the September party to take over the work until the return of the Nicholses. Those few months of the interim were strenuous indeed. It looked as though there would be no time whatever to prepare for my wedding.

Finally one morning Dr. and Mrs. Jameson came up and Dr. Jameson said, "Your Auntie," meaning Mrs. Jameson, the unlovable (?), "and I have talked things over and we have decided that we are not quite ready to let you kill yourself. So we are coming up here and

I am going to take over the Mission Accounts" (with scores of jungle schools, churches and Evangelists this was no sinecure) "and your Auntie will take over the housekeeping and thus relieve you a little and give you an opportunity to get ready to be married." In addition to his own work Dr. Jameson voluntarily assumed this added burden and Mrs. Jameson cheerfully left her own home in order to make a home for Miss Watson and me. What their coming just at that time meant to me, no words of mine can express.

I remember that during this period, shortly before Mr. Carson was due in Rangoon, a young Englishman called me out of the service one Sunday morning and told me that his stepmother was very ill and was constantly calling for me. I said I would go to her at once.

He hesitated a little and then said: "I think I should tell you that she has *cholera*. And if you are afraid or feel the least nervous I think you had better not go." Assuring him that I was not in the least afraid, I accompanied him to the home of his father, who was a sea captain who had recently married for his second wife a beautiful young English girl. She had only been a few months out from England. On Friday evening we had taken a long walk together and she was in abounding health and the gayest of spirits. She had only been sick a few hours, yet when I entered the room I would not have known her, so terrible are the ravages of that dread disease. She had not been told the nature of her disease, and when I came up to her bed she reached up, put her arms about my neck and drew me down to "kiss me for coming." The exertion caused her to vomit and it covered the front of my dress. From that moment I knew that I was liable to be a corpse any time within the next three or four days. I lifted a silent prayer for the bridegroom then approaching Calcutta.

After washing the stains from my dress I went back to the bedside of the sick woman and ministered to her until she died a few hours later. All night long I stayed with the corpse and helped prepare the beautiful body for burial. Returning to the Mission next morning, weary with the night's vigil and grieved for the loss of the sweet young life so far from her home and loved ones, in all probability I would soon have followed her had not Mrs. Jameson taken me immediately in hand. She went with me to my room, had me drop all of the clothing I had worn into a tub of boiling water which she had placed out of doors under my window, then gave me a hot bath with disinfectant, washed my hair, darkened my room, and put me to bed admonishing me not to get up until I was thoroughly rested and could sleep no longer. "For it would be a sad experience for a young missionary to come all the way from America and find no bride."

When the "young missionary" reached Calcutta he discovered that the trunk containing his wedding suit, and the wedding cake made by my dear mother's hands, had been left in England! It turned up some two or three months after we were married. Fortunately my dress was in another trunk and the party was detained in Calcutta long enough for Mr. Carson to have another suit made.

The bridegroom had expressed a desire to have a very quiet wedding. This also suited my wishes, but when I told the missionaries my plans they said it would never do, that the Karen Christians would feel terribly hurt if their "Mamma" should be married and they were not permitted to be present at the ceremony. So it transpired on the eventful morning of December 18, 1886, that Karen Christians flocked in from every direction and that instead of the quiet little wedding we had hoped for there were more than two thousand people present, fourteen of whom (including bride and groom) were white! The ceremony took place in the splendid Ko-tha-byu Hall, named for the first Karen Christian and built by the Karens themselves. Two native teachers who had been educated in America took charge of the decorating and with a large committee of students they converted the entire great hall into a bower of beauty. The great pillars were wound with garlands of green, and festoons of the beautiful Tha-bu-baw were caught from the center of the ceiling to the pillars at the sides. Loveliest ferns and crotons were artistically clumped on the broad rostrum, and dozens of pots of purest white lilies with their glossy green leaves, were arranged along the front. It seemed to me that no bride ever had a lovelier setting. The Mission House was connected with the Hall by a covered walk and this walk was spread with mats for the bridal party.

Mr. F. D. Phinney, for so many years Superintendent of our great Mission Press in Rangoon, was best man and Miss Watson was bridesmaid. Dr. Jameson, whom I think of as the most saintly man I ever knew, oh, so beautifully and tenderly performed the ceremony. The Karens sweetly sang an original hymn prepared for the occasion by the Karen pastor of the church—Saw Tay Naw—another saintly character of truly wonderful ability. ,

Under a beautiful arch in the Mission House congratulations were received, every Karen feeling in duty bound to shake hands with the bride. With that tremendous crowd it was a time-consuming performance, though facilitated by the crowd passing orderly in at one door and out at an opposite one. Long before the finish my white gloves were black, and my arm was lame for days afterwards.

This ceremony over, the white people passed into the "banquet hall," which Mrs. Jameson's dear hands and good taste had made very lovely. Small tables were laid, and beautifully decorated, for the guests. A large American flag, made by Mrs. Jameson and the bride, and a Union Jack were crossed at the head of the table prepared for the bridal party. The luncheon was daintily served and delicious. The Karen guests were furnished, by the bride, with a large beef, and I do not remember how many hogs—*they did the rest!* They had a fine feast of rice and curry and went home happy.

The day after the wedding was spent in packing our goods and getting them on board a steamer for Henzada, where we were to relieve the Thomases so they could take charge of the Zigon Burman Mission, as Mr. George's health made it imperative that they leave at once for America. This was only a temporary measure. Other arrangements were to be made as soon as possible so we might open up work among the Chins. We were to be with the elder Mrs. Thomas in Henzada. She was deeply interested in the Chins and with her Karen helpers had worked so effectually among them that the first Sunday we were in Henzada she had them called in from the jungle and Mr. Carson had the joy of baptizing thirteen adult converts.

The Thomases remained in Henzada just long enough to attend the Karen Association which was held in a near-by village. Sending bedding, clothing, food, dishes, curtains, hymn books, medicine, tracts and countless other things out on an ox cart the day before, we missionaries rode ponies out the next morning. The meetings were held under a great straw-covered shed prepared for the purpose and there were hundreds of people present. The entire day was taken up with meetings and eating!—and the night with singing. How they did sing! And they kept it up until two o'clock in the morning. But, frivolous as it may seem, the thing I remember best of that whole four days of meetings was the effect caused by Polly, a dear Karen girl in the Henzada School. Her father, known in the Mission as Chaucer (Chaw Ser) lived in the village where the Association was held. Polly wanted her father to be dressed up for the great occasion so she bought and took out to him a pair of cotton trousers. Now Chaucer had never worn trousers before and to Polly's discomfort and the amusement of the missionaries he appeared before the crowd, proud as a peacock, with his trousers *on hind side before!*

During our stay in Henzada, and both before and after the taking of Upper Burma by the British, the whole country was harassed by bands of dacoits, burning, looting and sacking villages. The Karens and Chins, almost to a man, were loyal to the British and consequently incurred the hatred of the Burmans. One morning as I sat in the Mission House a Chin woman with a hideous tattooed face staggered into the room, fell at my feet on the floor, dropped her head in my lap and sobbed pitifully. She was so utterly exhausted it was a long time before she could tell us her story. Then she told me her name was Ma Ba. She was a Christian and the little band of Christians in her village had met on Sunday morning to worship. While absent, their homes had been entered and looted and then set on fire. Seeing their homes burning they fled in terror into the jungle and had been wandering about for four days without food and a part of the time suffering agonies for water, trying to find their way to the Mission. They had little children with them who had to be carried; parties got separated while searching for water and they were in constant terror of being overtaken by the cruel dacoits and treated as one poor Karen woman was—bound to a tree, her clothes saturated with kerosene and burned alive. When finally they reached the Mission and safety the reaction was almost more than they could bear.

We remained in Henzada only three months, but how we learned to love dear old black-faced Ma Ba, who had, through such terrible suffering, led the little band of Christians to safety!

In the spring of 1887 Mr. Thomas (who knew more about the habitat of the Chins than any one else and who was deeply interested in their evangelization), Mr. Carson and myself were authorized by the Board to go up the country and search out the best place for establishing the new Mission. Accordingly we went up the Irrawaddy River, stopping at various places and making inquiries of officials and natives and gathering such data as was possible. In Thayetmyo there were a few Burman Christians and a small chapel where outstation work was carried on by Rev. E. O. Stevens of Prome. Furthermore, there were Chin villages on the opposite side of the river as well as along the foothills extending both north into unexplored regions and south to villages in which some religious work had been done. We therefore unanimously agreed upon Thayetmyo as the most strategic place for establishing the new Mission, and an application was sent in to the British Government for a grant of land for that purpose.

In company with the Deputy Commissioner, Mr. Carson carefully looked over all the available sites in or near the city and finally decided upon one just outside of the municipality. The Deputy Commissioner was amazed at his choice, exclaiming, "Why, that is nothing but a dump heap." But Mr. Carson saw the possibilities of the place and the beautiful compound evolved from the jungle "dump heap" proved the wisdom of his choice—beautiful "Jungle Lodge!"

As Dr. Stevens was obliged to go home on furlough we were asked to take charge of his work at Prome until a new man could be sent out. Prome being only a half day's trip by steamer from Thayetmyo, it was thought that we could oversee the work there while getting things started for the new Mission at Thayetmyo. This we undertook to do. We found everything in splendid condition in Prome so far as all details of the work were concerned. We had planned to put in every available hour while there upon the language of our Chins. But there was a large Burmese school which we had to superintend; and the pupils were so quarrelsome that we found it impossible, without any knowledge of their language, to discipline them with justice. We therefore gave ourselves with considerable determination to the study of Burmese. While we did not exactly rejoice over the number of quarrels we had to settle, we did feel thankful many times afterwards that *something* compelled us to familiarize ourselves with the dominant language of the country.

Some of the Prome Christians were among the finest characters I have known in Burma. Let me tell the story of one girl's life which has taught me many a useful lesson. A bright, clean young girl from a Christian family was lured away by the English captain of a river steamer and became his mistress. She had been forbidden to come on the Mission compound when we went to Prome, as we had some unusually attractive young ladies there and it was feared that others might be enticed into following her example. I sent for the girl to come and see me. In response to the summons she came, beautifully dressed and bejeweled, but a little shy as if uncertain how she would be received. I received her kindly but had a long plain talk with her. At first she resented it and was stubborn and angry. Then she said that the man was good and kind to her and gave her many beautiful presents; that she loved him and could not give him up. I did not ask her to give him up, but talked of what a terrible thing it was to bring reproach upon the name "Christian" where so few knew the matchless Christ—the One to whom all must look for salvation. Praying for guidance, I talked tenderly and sympathetically, not blaming her, but telling her how Christ had forgiven the woman taken in sin, saying that He did not condemn her, but for her to go and sin no more.

Suddenly she flung herself at my feet, buried her head in my lap and sobbed. I smoothed her hair with my hand, but said nothing. Presently she jumped up, rushed from the house and was gone. I did not see her again for weeks. But one afternoon she came again to my room, flung herself at my feet, hid her face in my lap and wept. She said she had been very unhappy since she left me and that she could not get away from a sense of her sin—it haunted her day and night. At last she had decided to give up the life she was leading and do what she knew to be right at whatever cost. She could not stay there where she was known. Would I help her to go to some other place where she could redeem her character? She was willing to do anything, *anything* if only she could get away from that awful sense of sin and shame. I wrote a letter to a missionary in Mandalay, told her the girl's story, said that I believed she was truly repentant and asked her to give her a chance to redeem herself, requesting that although she was unusually competent, not to put her forward, but to keep her in the background until she had proved her sincerity. She went to Mandalay. A great-hearted missionary dealt with her wisely and lovingly and she became one of the most efficient and best loved of all the Bible women I have known in Burma; she is still at her work going about from day to day among people in need of help, carrying sunshine and sympathy and hope and love into every house she enters—a marvelously beautiful character.

After she went to Mandalay I did not see her until she had been one of dear Miss Fredricksen's most loved and trusted helpers for years. When she saw me enter the room she rushed up to me, dropped her head on my shoulder and sobbed. When told of the joy it had given me to hear of the splendid life she was leading she said: "Yes, dear Mamma, I cannot thank you enough for helping me. I am very happy in my work but, oh, Mamma, I cannot forget. It is just like spilling ink on a white injie [jacket]—you can wash and wash and wash, but you can never get quite all the stain out." "No," I said, "it is not like that for the blood of Jesus Christ cleanseth from *all* sin. Though your sins be as scarlet, they shall be as white as snow."

We waited long weary months before we were able to get the grant for our land, but finally it came and work was begun on clearing and making it fit for human habitation. In the meantime a little son, whom we named Carl Hardin, was born to us, and Rev. and Mrs. H. H. Tilbe were sent out to take charge of the work in Prome.

Accordingly in the summer of 1888 we moved to Thayetmyo and the first Chin Mission was established. Mr. Carson built a dear little (temporary) bamboo house with mat walls and thatch roof in which we lived while building a more permanent dwelling. It was clean, cool and delightful, but very small. An English officer's wife who came to call said it was "like a veritable bit of fairy land" and in comparison with their big dark teak houses it was. We took with us four young men and two girls, all Chin Christians, to help us in both our temporal and spiritual work and to form the nucleus for a school which we hoped to open. The boys built a little bamboo house for themselves, but the girls were obliged to sleep in one of our three little rooms. In the largest room all of our meetings were held. We got on all right until the heavy rains came on, when the girls were obliged to stay in the house all of the time and when the excessive dampness ruined our clothing, spoiled our food, depressed our spirits and injured our health. While in Prome I had had Asiatic cholera and nearly lost my life. Here I had a very hard attack of pleurisy which gave my husband great anxiety and he wrought with almost superhuman effort to complete the building of a house suitable to protect the health of his family. We were building it of brick. He besought, begged, even bribed the contractor to make haste, but to no avail. Every few days every workman would be off his job on account of some feast, funeral, unlucky day or whatnot. Month after month dragged on. Finally the roof was put on. The timbers proved too heavy and crushed the walls so that practically the whole thing had to be done over again.

What my poor husband suffered during the building of that house would, it seemed to me, have made Job himself acknowledge defeat. But at last it was completed and occupied and soon after—March 30th, 1889—a second son, Max Howard, was born to us. No physician was in the place at that time, the Civil Surgeon having been transferred and the man to take his place having not yet arrived. Dr. Marie Cote, then of our Mission, had agreed to be with us at that time, but being offered charge of the Lady Dufferin Hospital in Rangoon just before she was to have come to us, and accepting, made it impossible for her to come. We were alone.

CHAPTER 9

FIRST RETURN TO AMERICA

Not long afterwards it was very evident to us that if I ever had any health it would be necessary for me to return to America for treatment. The Jamesons with whom I had come to Burma six years before, were both greatly broken in health and were to return to America in October. Arrangements were made for me to accompany them, leaving Mr. Carson to care for the new work alone.

In miserable health, in the company of two missionaries both sick, and with two babies, one twenty months and the other six months old, the long voyage ahead of me did not foster the hope of an ideal pleasure trip. Nor was it. We could only procure passage from Rangoon as far as Singapore. We went on board our steamer late at night as we were to sail when the tide favored very early the next morning. As we went through the dining room and past the pantry on the way to our cabins we saw the Indian servants washing up the dinner dishes. They sat on the floor with their feet stretched out. One had a dish pan in front of him and the other a cocoanut fiber door mat. There were stacks and stacks of dishes all about them. Some had been washed and some had not. It was hot and the men were perspiring furiously. A large pile of dishes had been washed and put to drain on the door mat and the men were wiping them on a very dirty table cloth, dragging it back and forth over their naked perspiring legs. The whole lot of dishes, washed and unwashed, were swarming with huge slimy cockroaches—the kind that leave a gooey trail behind them! Ugh! What an appetizer for the beginning of a sea voyage!

We went to our cabin and put the babies to bed. The mosquitoes were so thick—and hungry—that they drove us frantic. My husband remained on board most of the night helping me to keep mosquitoes and cockroaches off the babies so they could sleep. Of course when we got out to sea the mosquitoes vanished. Not so the cockroaches!

There were only two berths in my cabin—one above the other. When the second night came (I had sat up the first night fighting mosquitoes) I was nonplussed as to what to do about sleeping arrangements. I dared not put the babies in the upper berth lest they tumble out; nor did my state of health warrant my climbing up and down a number of times during the night to care for the children. Consequently, the first night my steamer rug was folded and spread on the floor for my bed; but the room was so small that, with trunks under the berth, it was impossible to straighten my limbs and I got up the next morning so stiff and lame from lying in a cramped position on the hard floor that some other arrangement seemed necessary. So the following night a steamer trunk was turned about, a rug put on top of it and there with my head sharing the pillow of the baby in the nearest end of the berth, I slept—or tried to—for six nights.

When we reached Singapore we found that a Blue Funnel freighter would be leaving for Manila via Hongkong within a few hours. If we waited for a passenger boat there was no telling how long it would be before we could get away. The freighter was designed to carry a very few passengers and there was just room for our party, so without even landing we took passage on her for Hongkong, transferring from one ship to the other. There were five or six English passengers and the service was English—everything in cabins and dining room was spotless. How good it was to have food that we felt was clean. During the eight preceding days I had not seen food without a mental vision of perspiring legs and swarming cockroaches. The only trouble about the new environment was that there was no passengers' deck and that the steamer had some sort of a patent arrangement for fanning the fire which blew the soot and cinders all over the little passages that answered for a deck and obliged us to stay inside the dining room. If by any chance the babies got beyond the threshold for a moment they looked like pickaninnies and required an immediate bath. As our course took us across the Equator the heat was intense and we found it hard to stay cooped up in a room so small that we could not move about and so hot that we fairly gasped for breath. After turning north it was better—and there were only six days of it anyhow.

When we arrived in the harbor of Hongkong Dr. Jameson went ashore at once, leaving us behind, to see what the prospect was for getting out of Hongkong for San Francisco. He found that the White-Star liner *Oceanic* would sail early the next morning and by transferring that night we would be able to get passage on her. This we arranged to do; but there was trouble about getting baggage from the hold and transference from one ship to the other so that it was two o'clock in the morning before we were able to get the babies to bed. When finally there was a place ready for them they could not sleep and that night is one long to be remembered. But the new cabin in this fine steamer! After the cramped quarters up to this stage of our voyage I wondered if Heaven could ever seem more glorious to me than did this large roomy cabin with an easy chair and a double bed. I simply reveled in it. When the babies finally got off to sleep near morning they slept on and I asked the stewardess to keep near the cabin while I took a bath and freed myself of the soot from the other boat. We were just passing out of the harbor into the open sea and encountered a squall. As I was stepping out of the bathtub the ship gave a lurch and I fell across the edge of the tub, fracturing two ribs. It was well for me that I had a large cabin and a double bed. Mrs. Jameson was confined to her bed with acute suffering. Dr. Jameson was almost as bad. There was a company of New York "society people" returning from the Paris Exposition whose wants were legion so that the stewardess could not give me much time with the children. Consequently day after day was spent in that blessed double bed with both children crawling over me and sitting upon me, while every breath was like the cut of a knife. But God "tempered the wind to the shorn lamb" for we were going with the wind made a record trip between Hongkong and San Francisco and, the only time in all the many sea voyages I have taken, *I was not seasick.*

Only once during that fourteen days' voyage was I on deck—and that was the night before landing and after the babies were in bed and asleep.

The thing that particularly presents itself when I think of the night and day in San Francisco is the fact that when we got ready to leave for the train the bunch of keys to suit-cases and trunks could not be found. We searched *everywhere*, and it was nearing time to leave. What should we do? Every pocket was turned inside out, every suit-case searched, but no keys. "Let us ask the Lord to help us find them," said Mrs. Jameson. We all knelt and Dr. Jameson in his trusting childlike way told the Lord of our trouble and asked him for help. As we arose from our knees we saw the bunch of keys on the top of a wardrobe where they had been placed to be out of the reach of the babies, and then forgotten.

When we left San Francisco—this was November—vegetation was still green and beautiful. When we looked out of the car window in the morning, snow was falling and everything was covered with a mantle of ermine. The two little boys had never seen anything like it before, and with eyes filled with shining delight the older one cried out, "See! Mamma, see! Sugar, sugar!" When we got further on the "sugar" was so deep that we were greatly delayed and found upon our arrival in Denver that the train with which we hoped to connect had been gone for two hours. So near home after all those years of absence and yet obliged to stay in Denver until morning!

We were told that the hotel to which we had been recommended was "quite near" to the station, so though it was after dark, we started out on foot to find it. I carried one baby and led the other, with a traveling bag and various wraps on my arm, and we trudged through "sugared" streets until it seemed that I must certainly give up and sink down upon the street in exhaustion. Dr. Jameson, laden with grips, was forging on ahead expecting every moment to see the hotel. Mrs. Jameson, really too sick to be on her feet at all and equally heavy laden, was making desperate efforts to keep up with him. We brought up the rear, reminding one of immigrants arriving at Ellis Island. It must have been more than a mile that we traveled before reaching our hotel. It seemed like ten. Next morning we took a bus and made the trip with less difficulty. All day long the baby was carsick. He lay in my lap, white as a ghost, moaning pitifully. A sympathetic man who sat near me insisted every time the train stopped on my turning the baby over to him and going in search of soothing syrup. My refusing to do so branded me as a heartless mother and dried up all his springs of human kindness. He continually talked to other passengers of how the poor little fellow suffered, how easy it would be to comfort him and how persistently his mother refused to give him soothing syrup. How my fingers ached to chuck him out of the car window—so absolutely human are some missionaries.

We were to reach home that night and an hour or two before we were due, as our train stopped at a division, my brother and sister came aboard, having come to meet us. Oh, the relief of it! Time does not obliterate the feeling. I draw a sigh of satisfaction every time I think of it.

During this visit to the homeland I remained in America just ten months. People everywhere treated me with the utmost kindness. I got the necessary medical and surgical treatment and regained my health. Leaving the babies with my sister, I attended the National Anniversaries in Chicago, where I met a number of other missionaries and thoroughly enjoyed the meetings. Not being on the program I had not expected to speak, but as the one to represent Burma failed to appear I was called upon at the last moment to take her place.

In the autumn (1890) in company with a party of new missionaries I returned with my two little ones via England and Calcutta to Burma. Seasick every day and the children needing constant amusement and attention, the entire voyage recurs to me as one endless nightmare, only made endurable by the kind thoughtfulness of some of our party and the amusing pranks of the little ones. Carl insisted on walking the deck with "Auntie Gertie" and calmly invited "Gimmore" (Gilmore—who afterwards married "Auntie Gertie") to walk with some one else. Max would wake up in the middle of the night and cry because he "wanted Uncle Mosier" who had been so kind in entertaining him when I went to meals.

One day there was a very heated argument among the men; the tension was high and nearing a break, when Carl came running across the deck. One of the men turned and said, "Well, Carl, what do you know about it?" Carl paused, tilted his head to one side and said, "Know beanth," [beans] and ran on. They all laughed, the tension was eased, and the day saved.

CHAPTER 10

MA WINE AND MA PU

During my absence Mr. Carson had built a Boys' Dormitory and gathered a nice little school of boys; but there being no lady missionary no effort had been made to get girl pupils. A fine Karen Christian young man from Henzada was put in charge of the school. On my return we built a small Girls' Dormitory and made a special effort to get girls into the school.

As the people had no way of computing time, except the Robinson Crusoe method, before opening a term of school, preachers and teachers were sent out to the various villages to gather in the pupils. On one such occasion a preacher went to a village from which we had never had a pupil and of which not one of the inhabitants could read or write. He spent the night in the home of the village chief and in the evening talked to the assembled family of the mission and the wonderful things taught there—taught even to *girls!* The daughter of the chief, a twelve-year-old girl, listened with eager shining eyes. When the preacher ceased talking, "I am going to that school," she said. "You are *not going*," her mother replied; "the first thing we would hear would be that you were worshiping the foreign God." "Those who go are not *compelled* to worship Him," the preacher assured them. "Then I am going," said the girl. "Why not let her go?" said the father, who was an unusually intelligent man. "No one in this village can read and write and sing." The preacher seeing his advantage used his most persuasive powers, but the mother bitterly opposed. The girl, with the father on her side, was jubilant and kept saying, "I am going, I am going." Finally the mother said, "Well, if you go, remember you are not to worship the foreign God." With this Ma Wine felt that the battle was won and the next morning in company with the preacher she started for the Mission. She proved a very bright and lovable girl and made fine progress in school. She had her daily Bible lesson with the others and attended services regularly. Early in the second year of her stay with us she was brightly and beautifully converted, and oh, how she prayed for her parents! She could not write and tell them of her new-found joy because there was no one in her village who could read. But some people passing through her village told her parents that Ma Wine had become a Christian. They were very angry and sent her word that if it were true she need never return home for they would not receive her.

She felt bad and prayed harder—but we had no happier student in all our school. As the long vacation approached I called her and said: "What shall you do, Ma Wine? You know your parents have sent word that you cannot come home. Do you want to remain at the Mission during the vacation?" "Oh, no," said she, "I am going to my father's village, even if I can't go home, and I am going to stay there and preach until my father becomes a Christian." Her mother had been so bitter that her faith was not strong enough to dare hope for her.

She *did* return to her father's village and went to the home of a friend. She was an unusually bright and attractive girl and had a very sweet voice. She had learned to read and to sing and had taken books, hymns and tracts home with her. These she used in entertaining her friends until her wonderful accomplishments became the talk of the village, and people came from all the near-by villages to hear her read and sing and tell marvelous stories she had learned at the Mission. Finally her father could stand it no longer. He came and said, "Ma Wine, you had better come home." This filled her heart with joy. Her father was so proud of her accomplishments that whenever a chief came from another village he called her out and had her read and sing for him. *A girl who could read!* And how beautifully she sang!

The upshot of it all was that before the end of the vacation Ma Wine brought both her father and mother to the Mission to be baptized. Her father, besides being village chief, was a man of great influence and before long, through his efforts, a school and church were built up in his village where formerly there had never lived a Christian and where no one in the village could either read or write.

On another occasion when the children were brought in for the opening of school there were so many that all could not be provided for. Among them there was a new girl who presented an unusually repulsive appearance. She was very dirty, wore almost no clothing, her hair was matted to her head and alive with vermin. Furthermore, she had a very large ugly scar on one side of her face which made her repellent.

My husband came in after the arriving of the last lot of prospective pupils and said that it would be simply impossible to care for them all in our cramped quarters and that some of them must be sent back to their jungle homes. He said that we must try to keep at least one from each village represented so as to create an interest in as many villages as possible. I immediately replied: "Well, then send that hideous-looking girl back to Thanoogin—we have others from that village." "Do you mean the girl with the scar on her face?" asked my husband. "Yes, if you have to send anybody back for pity's sake let her be one of them. I hate to have to see her around," I heartlessly answered. Carl was playing in the room and heard the conversation; he looked up quickly and said, "Oh, that is Ma Pu! Please, Papa, don't send her away. I like Ma Pu." "But, Carl, we can't keep all who come and surely she is not a very promising-looking specimen," his father answered. "Oh, Papa, please don't send her away. *I think she will come out.* Please, please, let her stay," he begged. The child was so insistent that it was finally arranged for her to stay. After a good soap bath—probably the first in her ten years of life—her hair soaked in kerosene to kill the vermin, well washed and neatly combed, and fresh clean clothing on she looked like a different person. She started in to school and proved to have a very sweet voice and an unusually bright mind. She made remarkable progress and being very sunny and sweet of disposition she won her way into all hearts. Carl's loyalty and love for her never abated, and she frequently accompanied the children in their walks. Their father had got for the little boys a little red "express wagon" from America. Ma Pu was called to admire it and take them for a ride. They passed a cow with a young calf. She charged them, but Ma Pu threw herself between the children and the cow. She was tossed again and again on the horns of the infuriated animal, always managing to protect the children until some men with bamboo poles rushed to the rescue. The poor girl was terribly bruised and battered and bleeding and her clothes torn to shreds, but the children were uninjured. We felt that she had heroically and unselfishly saved their lives and we took her into our own home. Here she remained until she finished school. She made her grades each year and passed the Government examinations in music, needlework, weaving and lace making, besides the regular branches taught. After finishing school we kept her on to help with the work and she became engaged to a fine Christian young man.

Several years later I was compelled to take little Max to America in order to save his life, and we were at our wits' ends to know what provision could be made for some one to do the work I had been doing.

Although it was—and is—the policy of our Mission Boards that unmarried women should have charge of the station-school work, we had never had a single lady assistant in our work for the Chins. We had gathered a goodly number of girls and had built a dormitory for them. *Somebody* must have them in charge during my absence. We had discussed the matter over and over again, but could see no solution to the problem.

One evening Ma Pu came in and with a little embarrassed laugh said, "I came to offer my services. I don't want you to suppose that I think I could ever take Mamma's place. I know I could not. But I know how she likes to have things done and I am willing to do my best until some one else can be sent from America or until Mamma's return." "But, Ma Pu, you are to be married. What would Maung Taung say?" said my husband. "He can wait," she said. "Please try me. I will do my best." And so that also was settled. Ma Pu stayed by the work until my return, looking after the buying of food for the girls, having charge of their dormitory and superintending the washing, ironing, cooking, cleaning and sewing, and changing of the different groups of girls each week so all would learn the different kinds of work. This she did so efficiently that Mr. Carson said he did not know how he ever could have carried on the work without her. After my return she was married and she and her Christian husband went to a distant village and opened up a school among the untaught and unevangelized of their race. They have done a great work, winning the confidence and love of the entire community and leading many to the feet of the Master. We felt that Ma Pu did indeed "come out" and amply justified Carl's faith in her and his pleading on her behalf.

CHAPTER 11

JUNGLE TRIPS

Jungle travel in an oxcart with solid wheels and no springs was so hard for a woman and children that my husband got a spring wagon out from America, hoping in this way to be able to take me and the children with him to visit the villages in the foothills with something less of discomfort. We tried making a trip with the spring wagon and ponies but found the road so rough it was terrible. Dr. Tilbe made the trip with us on horseback. We had an oxcart for our bedding, dishes, food box, books, medicines, camp chairs, clothing, horse feed, etc. We came to a stream that must be forded. Dr. Tilbe crossed first to see if it would be safe to attempt driving through. The water came up to his pony's sides but he called back that it was all right. We drove down a steep bank into deep water, the wheel struck a rock, and Mr. Carson and the two boys on the front seat were pitched headlong into the water. The lines caught on the axle, wound around and pulled the ponies to a standstill in midstream. We on the back seat were not thrown out. Never have I felt so utterly helpless. All three of my dear ones went to the bottom but soon came up again. Carl somehow reached shallow water and scrambled out, saying as he did so, "Mamma, my sooz (shoes) are all muddy!" as if that were the only matter of particular interest. When I saw Max's yellow curls sink the second time I was on the point of leaping in, but his father, who had struck a stone and was somewhat stunned, was, nevertheless, instantly to the rescue and soon had both boys safely in the wagon. Unwinding the reins from the axle was not an easy matter but was finally accomplished and we drove on to the village with gratitude welling up in our hearts because the accident had not been even more serious.

Dr. Tilbe, not dreaming of any trouble, had ridden on to find a suitable place for us to camp. He was surprised enough when he saw the three soaked members of our party and was told of our experiences. I had taken a quilt, a large bath towel, cushions and some crackers, knowing that we would get in ahead of the cart and thinking to give the children a bath, the crackers and a nap before the cart came with our things. It was well that we had these things for, taking the wet clothing off the children, I had not a dry thing to put on them—had to make them lie down on the quilt on the floor of the zayat and let me cover them with the towel while their clothes dried in the sun.

This accident happened about ten o'clock in the morning and we waited until after dark for the cart to come with our food, clothing, bedding, etc. The cartman had followed our trail, tried to cross the stream at the same place, struck the same rock and his whole load had been pitched into the stream. They were hours rescuing things and when they finally came, books, bedding, clothing, sugar, flour, bread, *everything* was soaking wet. We had been all day without food and were ravenously hungry. We satisfied ourselves as best we could on condensed milk and canned fruit and went to bed on the one dry quilt, for four of us, spread on the bamboo floor. We had planned to move on early the next morning, but were obliged to camp a day in order to dry our things.

Arriving at home, we were busy for several days preparing for another trip to our Association. This time we made the first part of the journey by river steamer, traveling a day's journey down the Irrawaddy on a cargo boat to Myanaung. Here we camped over night and early in the morning engaged an oxcart to take us out to Thanoogin where the meetings were to be held. We made a shade over the cart with a quilt which we tied to bamboos which we had bound with *hnees* (strips of bamboo) to the four corners of the cart. Putting the children in the cart we ourselves walked for several hours. During the hottest part of the day we rested under some trees and ate our lunch. The school boys who were with us clambered like monkeys up some cocoanut trees and soon brought us fresh cocoanut water to drink, which we found both refreshing and delicious.

Tired, dusty, hot and hungry, we reached Thanoogin in the early evening and were most cordially welcomed by the Christians. They had built a little bamboo house for our accommodation. And though it had no furniture and we had to sit and sleep on the floor, it was fresh and clean and made us a very comfortable abiding place for the week of our stay. We had fine meetings, settled several quarrels and baptized quite a number of converts. The meetings over we started shortly before sunset on our homeward trip, intending to travel to the first camping place while cool, and go on to Myanaung in the morning. Putting the children into the cart, we started it on ahead, we following on foot with a large number of Christians who escorted us outside the village and for a mile or two on our way.

Soon after we had said good-by to them, and as it was growing dusk, we noticed that the cart had stopped, and we heard altercations and threats. Hurrying forward, we saw a cart halted immediately in front of ours. Three drunken Burmans were in the cart, one flourishing a large knife and ordering our cartman to give the road. The unwritten law, known to all the natives, was that carts going towards the river, usually loaded, had the right of way; and that carts returning, usually empty, should always turn out for them. Our cartman was arguing his rights while the drunken Burmans, flourishing knives, were calling down all sorts of maledictions upon his head. As we rushed up from behind our cart it startled the oxen facing us and they bolted into the jungle taking the infuriated Burmans with them. The oxen ran astride a tree, jerked free from the cart and fled wildly into the depths of the jungle. The men were in a perfect frenzy of anger. They threatened us with the most horrible death and screamed and swore in a way to make one's blood turn cold. My husband said very quietly, "You are too drunk to realize what you are saying. You would better rescue your oxen or they will get so far into the jungle you will not be able to find them." Realizing the danger of this, they started off as fast as their wabbly legs would take them, calling back invectives as long as we could hear them and saying that they would overtake us and burn us alive before morning. Our cartman was terrified lest they carry out their threat and suggested that we leave the main road and make a detour which would probably throw them off our track. This we did, driving over a rough unknown road until late into the night. About eleven o'clock we came to a little zayat—floor with a roof over it—and stopped to rest our oxen and get a little sleep if possible. We gave the children some crackers and condensed milk, spread our quilts on the floor and lay down to rest until two o'clock. My husband, not knowing what might happen, dared not sleep at all, but kept watch in order that I might be able to throw off anxiety and get some rest. From sheer exhaustion I soon slept soundly. At two o'clock we got the children up and were soon on the road again. We hoped by starting so early to reach Myanaung before the sun was dangerously hot. We were off the main road and wandered about for hours in the general direction we wanted to go vainly trying to find it. At last we reached a road which the cart man assured us he knew to be the right one. Once on this road Mr. Carson said he would hasten on ahead, find a place for us to stop and have some breakfast ready on our arrival.

He had not been gone more than a half hour when "Max Galay" [Little Max], sitting by the driver, reached forward to prod the oxen with a sharpened bamboo as he had seen the cartman do, and pitched headlong just in front of the heavy wheel, which ran over him. We were traveling over a road where the dust was well-nigh a foot deep and this fact doubtless saved the child's life, as it pressed him down into the dust instead of crushing his tender little body. As soon as I saw him fall I leaped from the side of the cart, my dress caught on the pickets and I was jerked out on my head so that I saw stars and my dress was torn into ribbons. Max was strangling and choking with the dust which filled his eyes, nose, mouth, throat and ears. I could not tell how badly he was hurt and was in agony lest he were dying. No water was near but I saw a little hut in the middle of a rice field about a quarter of a mile away, where children were jerking strings which had leaves tied at intervals, and were fastened to posts in the corners of the field, to frighten the birds from the ripening rice. I rightly judged the children would have a chattie of drinking water and sent the cartman in all haste to bring it. While he was gone I wiped the dust as best I could from the poor little eyes and throat and undressed and examined the little body to see if I could tell how badly it was hurt. The mark of the wheel was plainly visible across the back of his shoulders just below the neck. He seemed stunned and scarcely cried at all—just moaned pitifully. Would he die before I could reach Myanaung? Oh, the agony of that day and how I prayed!

Finally the man came with water and I gave the little boy a drink and washed the dust from his eyes, ears and throat. This revived him greatly and after fixing an awning with a quilt over the top of the cart, I made him as comfortable as I could and got in the cart by his side to watch him, for I was not sure how serious the accident might prove to be. We had been delayed so long that it was growing late and the heat was becoming intense. The dust was deep and the oxen traveled slower and slower. First I had the native preacher get out to lighten the load and help the cartman urge the oxen on. But finally they stopped altogether and the cartman said they were tired and wanted water and we would have to camp till evening. I told him that we *must* go on, that it was dangerous to our lives to be so long out in the sun; furthermore I did not know how badly the little boy was hurt and *must* get him to a doctor. I got out of the cart and had the nurse girl do likewise to further lighten the load, and we started on again. But soon the oxen slowed down and almost stopped and I summoned the preacher and the nurse and all three of us waded through the dust and pushed on the back of the cart in order to keep it going, for miles. Finally the cartman called out, "There comes the Saya!" and sure enough beyond the cloud of dust we were making we saw the white man's topee (big pith hat) looming near. Blessed sight! I rushed forward to meet him, the strips of my torn skirt fluttering, my whole being gray with dust, and streams of perspiration chasing one another through the dirt on my face. I dropped my head into its rightful place of refuge—a place that had never failed to bring comfort and peace—and sobbed and sobbed before I was able to tell what had befallen us and why we were so late. Mr. Carson had reached Myanaung, found a zayat for us to occupy and prepared breakfast, but still we did not come. He grew uneasy as the sun got higher and hotter and walked out several miles to meet us. Seeing nothing of us he returned, thinking we must have come another road and expecting to find us on his return. When we were not there he was truly alarmed and hastened back by the other road which was much longer and which of course we had taken. He met us about two miles from the town and soon had us comfortably settled in the zayat to await our steamer. When we showed the "blue print" on our little man's shoulders the doctor said if the wheel had struck him one-half inch higher up it would certainly have killed him. So in our gratitude that he was not seriously injured we forgot the hard experiences in grateful thanksgiving and reached home in safety two days later.

CHAPTER 12

KO SO, KO MIN, AND MAUNG TUN

One morning Ko So, a hard-drinking Chin man, who was the father of a large family, a man to whom the gospel had often been preached and who had been urged without any apparent response to put his children into the Mission School, came to the Mission House. He stood about, carrying something under his blanket, for some time before making his errand known. Finally he opened his blanket and took out an alabaster idol about eighteen inches long, very heavy and very white, and held it out to the Missionary saying, "I want to give this to you. I have no further use for it." "Why, what do you mean?" asked the missionary. "Well, it's like this," he said. "For many years I have had this god in the forks of a tree, and I have gone out just at dawn every morning and prostrated myself before it in worship, but it has brought me no peace. You have told me of another God who gives help and comfort and salvation, but he wants his followers to be sober and honest and truthful. I thought for a long time I could not give up liquor. But at last I have decided to worship the God of whom you have told me. I am drunk most of the time, I have no peace of heart, and my children are all going wrong. I want to put them into school. I want to be a Christian. In proof of my sincerity I have brought you the god I have worshiped all my life. It has brought me neither help nor comfort. Take it and do with it as you please." That idol was used for a door stop in the Thayetmyo Mission until we overheard some one say, "See, they worship Buddha too! There is his image." After which it was no longer in evidence.

The man straightened up, quit drinking, put his children into school and before long was baptized. He could read Burmese, having lived among the Burmans, and day after day he put in his spare time on the study of the Bible. He, after a time, became a preacher among his people. He was a faithful and valued worker all his life, but to show the difficulty in eliminating false ideas let me relate an incident which I happen to remember.

A Burman was greatly in need of a little money. He came to the Missionary wishing to borrow, and told his troubles. The Missionary, having made a rule not to loan money to the natives, finally agreed to advance the money if he would haul him two loads of wood by a certain date. The Burman received the price of the two loads of wood and went away happy. The date for the delivery of the wood came, but no wood. After waiting for a long time and being in need of the wood, Ko So was sent to see about it. It was promised but not brought. Again and again he went with the same result. Finally one day he came with his face beaming and said, "Well, Samo, this time I got it. The wood is coming!" "Good! How did you manage it, Ko So?" said the Teacher. He chuckled and said: "He had to raise more money and I told him you would pay cash for it." "But I won't. I have already paid for it long ago as you know. Why did you tell him I would?" "Of course you won't pay for it," he said smilingly. "I knew you wouldn't, but I couldn't get it any other way—and he owed it to you." "But you lied to him, Ko So. Here you have been a preacher for years teaching that it is wrong to lie and now you have been lying yourself. I would not have believed it," said the Missionary. "Was that lying—when he owed you the wood? I couldn't get it any other way," he said, "but I didn't mean to lie." And the poor old fellow actually shed tears. "Shall we do evil that good may come? God forbid!" quoted the Missionary.

Two of this man's sons became preachers and three others became teachers in Mission schools. His only daughter went to Rangoon to the Lady Dufferin Hospital and trained as a nurse and returned to minister to the suffering sisters of her race—women who because of their ignorance of hygiene and medicine, believing all pain and suffering to be caused by angry spirits, go through absolutely unnecessary suffering beyond the power of my pen to portray.

Ko Min was an old priest who presided at heathen feasts and led in incantations. He was usually maudlin with drink, but when sober was a man of unusual intelligence. He heard the gospel, believed, and was baptized. He was a man of great influence among the people and he traveled without salary year in and year out through sun and through rain, with the Missionary, admonishing the people to accept the Word of Life. He gave up drink and developed into one of the most lovable Christian characters I have ever known. He was the Missionary's constant companion and friend and when he was stricken by the disease that proved fatal we took him into our own home and ministered to him as to a brother beloved—which he truly was.

One morning he said to my husband: "Samo, I think Jesus is calling." "Yes," said Mr. Carson. "I think he is, and if you have anything to attend to, any messages to leave, you had better attend to it now while your mind is clear." "I am going to Jesus. It is all right. I would like to talk to the school boys," he said. We called them in until they filled the room. Never have I heard a more beautiful talk than he gave them. He begged them to be true to Christ that they might have the joy that was his when death came. Begged them to meet him in heaven. Then he said to the Missionary: "Samo, pray." My husband prayed, oh, so tenderly. Then Ko Min said, "Let's sing, 'Oh, Think of the Home Over There.'" With choking voices and streaming eyes we tried to sing, the dear old man joining in the chorus. When we had finished he said: "I am tired now. I want to sleep." The boys passed quietly out and a little later Ko Min was in "The Home Over There," where I confidently expect him to be among the first to greet me when I reach the heavenly shore.

On one occasion when Mr. Carson and Dr. Tilbe made a preaching tour together they went to a village which neither of them had ever visited before. They were treated with great rudeness. A large crowd gathered to hear them, but they were so noisy and created so much disturbance that they were obliged after repeated trials to give up long before they had completed their message, and return to the bamboo house where they were to spend the night. The crowd followed them and stoned the house and hooted insults after they had entered. During the night the house was broken into and their suitcases were stolen and burned. They found the charred remains not far from the house the next morning. Writing me the next day Mr. Carson told me of the treatment they had received and said they were shaking the dust of the place from their feet and hoped never to return.

The following year he was out one day mending a fence and called one of the school boys to help him. As they worked and chatted he said to the boy: "Maung Tun, where did you first hear the Gospel? I don't believe I ever heard you say." "Do you remember the time you and teacher Tilbe were stoned by Burmans and had your suitcases stolen and burned?" he asked. "Yes, I am not likely to forget that experience," Mr. Carson replied. "Well, it was that night that I first heard about Christ," he replied. "After the crowd dispersed I lay all night long looking up at the stars wondering if what you told us could be true. I could not sleep. Could it be possible, I wondered, that the white people's God really cared for the Chins and wanted them to love him? I thought and thought and thought. I could not get away from it. The next day I heard of some of my own race who were Christians and decided to go and see them. They lived two or three days' distant, but I went to their village determined to find out what they knew about this strange new religion. They told me all they could, but advised me to go to the Mission where they would explain things more fully. I was an orphan, there was nothing to hinder and so I came and entered school and found Christ." That boy became a very effective preacher of the gospel and led many people into the kingdom of God. What a lesson this incident was to us! A time when earnest seed sowing seemed absolutely wasted, yet overruled by God to bear most precious fruit. "My word shall not return unto me void." "In due season ye shall reap if ye faint not."

CHAPTER 13

QUEER CUSTOMS AND THRILLING EXPERIENCES

It was the custom of our southern Chins to cremate the dead. Building up a pile of wood in the jungle, the body was placed upon it and the fire started. As soon as it began to burn the people returned, wailing, to their homes. The following day the friends of the deceased went to the place of burning, gathered up the ashes and any remaining unburned portions of the body that might have escaped the dogs and wild animals, and putting them into a chattle (burnt clay jar) they went with chanting and ceremony and buried the jar with its contents under a sacred tree. Seeing one of the processions one day I asked one of the Christian women who had died. "Oh, they are just deceiving the gods," she replied. "How can they do that?" I asked. She explained that often when one became very sick they would make a mud image of him, give it his name, say that he was dead and go through all the funeral rites even to the burying of the ashes. The sick man was given a new name and nobody must ever call him by the old one. Thus the evil spirits would think that he was dead and, ceasing to trouble him, he would of course recover. Or if he failed to do so it was because some one had inadvertently called him by his old name and the spirits had learned they were being deceived and had therefore caused his death.

On our Thayetmyo field the climate was very hot, and troublesome insects and reptiles were abundant. At the beginning of the rains the heavy warm showers brought them out in large numbers. The flying white ants would rise from the ground in clouds; and during the first few evenings of their coming out we would have to go to bed, or get under our mosquito nets, to get away from them, for they would swarm about the lights in myriads and, losing their wings, drop to the floor. I noticed the girls coming in and placing pans of water under the lamps and in this way catching quarts of the insects. In reply to my inquiry as to what they were doing with them, "Oh, we parch them and eat them," they said. "They are delicious."

One hot day an Indian woman was cutting grass on our compound. She was bitten by a cobra and her blood being very hot she died within a few moments. Not long after we were all standing in the back yard playing with a little pet monkey when a cobra darted across the well-swept yard. Mr. Carson glanced about but seeing no weapon, and fearing to lose the chance of ridding the place of so dangerous a guest, rushed after it, took good aim and crushed its head with his heel. Not long afterwards the nurse was out walking with the little boys. Seeing a cobra in the road, Carl started after it in hot pursuit. The nurse had barely time to grab his clothing and jerk him back exclaiming as she did so, "Why, Carl, don't you know that is a cobra? What are you doing?" "I was going to kill it—the way Papa did," he answered. "Now you've let it go and it will bite somebody and he will die," he said reproachfully.

Being in the dry belt, our house was not built high up from the ground like most houses of the country, but the lower rooms at the back were near the ground level. One evening after a heavy rain we killed four centipedes and two scorpions *in the house!* But strange as it may seem in all the ten years and more that we were there none of us was ever injured by these poisonous creatures, except that I was once stung by a scorpion.

On one occasion while returning to Burma, going through the Suez Canal we had a fine view of Mt. Sinai—usually lost in haze—and I called the children to me and pointed it out, telling them that it was the mountain on which God had given the Ten Commandments, written on stone, to Moses, and that the Commandments had afterwards been printed in Bibles just as we had them printed at the Mission Press; and that they must always remember they had seen the mountain where God gave the tables of stone.

Carl was very much impressed by the fact that he had seen the mountain where God gave the tables of stone to Moses. Later, in talking with a Hindu gentleman, he delivered quite a sermon about his religion and told the Hindu it was the true religion. The Hindu said: "How do you know your religion is true?" "Why, it is in the *Bible*," said Carl. "But you don't know where your Bible came from," replied the Hindu. "Yes, I do," said Carl. "My Mamma showed me the very mountain where God gave it to Moses, written on stone, and Moses gave it to Mr. Phinney [our Mission Press Superintendent] and Mr. Phinney printed it into books."

Once while in the jungle my husband went out for an early Sunday morning walk. The path led to an almost perpendicular cliff of great height, but flat on the top. There was a path detouring around it, but he decided to attempt to climb it to get the view. With great difficulty he clambered up its side until, hot and perspiring but triumphant, he grasped the top layer of stone and drew himself up. His blood curdled as he saw a huge cobra little more than a foot from his hand basking in the morning sun. What should he do? To go on meant certain death. To loose his hold and drop on the stones below also meant death—or what in that isolated place would be worse than death—broken bones and mangled body. Scarcely daring to breathe, he lowered his head below the surface of the stone and prayed for help. Carefully drawing himself up again, he saw the cobra gliding down the opposite side of the cliff. Quickly gaining the top and standing, tremblingly, where the thing of death had been only a moment before, he praised God for answered prayer.

While on a long jungle trip where exposure and hardships were encountered to an unusual degree I was taken with a fever, and running rather a high temperature, my husband was very anxious to get me home, where I could have a doctor. In his anxiety for me he started traveling in the afternoon before the sun was low enough to be really safe for the children. The result was that when we reached home six-year-old Carl had a fever caused by the sun on his back, which was much worse than mine. He went into terrible convulsions and not daring to wait for the doctor's arrival I had him put into a hot bath—which for that kind of fever was just the *wrong* thing to do. When the doctor came he looked very serious saying that it was ice and not hot water that was needed. Mr. Carson went to the British Officers' Club, where they sometimes got ice at great expense by rail and boat from Rangoon. Fortunately they had some for an intended dinner party and generously gave it all. The doctor stayed and worked over the little man all night, keeping his head in an ice pack. But the next day the convulsions returned and we began to lose hope. Dr. Tilbe, our nearest missionary neighbor, who lived a half day's travel distant by steamer from us, was telegraphed for and came by the first boat. I was too ill myself to remember how many days the little fellow lay so terribly ill, but I know the day came when they laid him on the bed by my side that I might look upon the dear face again before the soul took flight. The forehead, arms and legs were cold and damp. The kind and fine English doctor stood by the side of the bed and with eyes full of tears said, "I have done all I could, Mrs. Carson. I loved the little chap and would give my own life to save his if I could." He rallied a little after that, but the doctor told Mr. Carson and Dr. Tilbe that if his temperature came up again *nothing* could save him, and that he expected him to pass away about midnight. Dr. Tilbe insisted on Mr. Carson going out for a little fresh air as he was very weary from loss of sleep, constant nursing and heart-wringing anxiety. He begged him to stay away from the sick room for at least an hour saying that he needed to "get hold of himself" in order to meet bravely what must come during the night. Reluctantly he went out. The child's temperature was taken every half hour. When Dr. Tilbe took it, it had begun to rise. With its going up our hopes went down. In about an hour Mr. Carson returned. He came in with radiant face. I shall never forget the expression of it or my wonder at it. He came straight to my bed and without any questions about the child he said, "Laura, he is going to live. God has given him back to us." This he said in an exultant voice and without a suspicion of doubt. "Oh, Arthur, don't, don't deceive yourself. You do not know—*his temperature is going up again!* And you know what the doctor said," I replied, fearing this renewed hope would make it all the harder for him to meet that which I felt must come.

There was a little white unused pagoda at the top of the hill back of our house. "Never mind," he said. "I never before went to a pagoda to pray, but I went this time and I prayed as I never prayed before and God has given me perfect assurance that our little boy will live. I *know* he has given him back to us," he said. He then went and took the temperature again. "Still rising," he said to my inquiring look, "but he is going to live. I feel perfectly certain of it," and the glow never left his face. A half hour later the temperature was taken again. "Dropped half a degree," he exclaimed exultantly. Another half hour and "Gone down a whole degree," was the report brought to my bed. And so it went on through the night gradually going lower and lower until by morning he was subnormal and very, very weak, but he dropped off into a natural sleep and slept restfully until the doctor came. "Why, what does this mean?" said the doctor going up to the bed. "Nothing but a miracle could have kept the child alive through the night. I did not expect for a moment to find him alive." "God answers prayer. He has given him back to us," said Mr. Carson reverently.

Gradually Carl recovered and was his happy self again, but he was years in America before the fever was entirely out of his system.

The following year Max was taken with typhoid fever. He was very, very ill. We watched over him day and night distraught between hope and fear for thirty-one days. Again we wired the Tilbes of our trouble and this time they both came, Mrs. Tilbe taking charge of the housekeeping and Dr. Tilbe looking after the work, thus freeing us to give our whole time to the care of our little one. We had a kind and efficient doctor. Indeed, I cannot say enough in praise of the English doctors in Burma. In all the serious illnesses in our family during the many years of our stay in that land not *one of pure British blood* would ever take one farthing for his service to the Mission, and he served us—native Christians and all—to the very best of his ability.

After thirty-one days, when the fever broke, our good doctor said that as soon as he got strength enough to be moved we must take our little boy to America. Mr. Carson suggested that I, who also needed a change, take him to Darjeeling or some of the hill stations in India. But the doctor said that he felt nothing but the long sea voyage and complete change would save his life and that I, also, needed a change to the homeland. Mr. Carson's furlough was long overdue, he having been nine years in the country without change except for one vacation of three weeks at the seashore. We planned and prayed and wrote letters and sent telegrams, but there seemed to be no possible provision to be made for our work so we could all go home together. It was finally decided that Mr. Carson would "stay by the stuff" until some one for the work could be sent out from America, and that I must take Max Galay and go without him. But what about Carl? With my own health so poor and with Max so ill and needing my constant care, Mr. Carson felt that I ought not to have the extra care that taking him would entail. At first we had had no thought but that he would go and had talked freely in his presence of the trip. He was greatly elated and talked continually about going to "The 'Merica." And "The 'Merica" to them was a synonym for Heaven. We talked the matter over one night after the children were asleep and Mr. Carson decided that he would broach the subject of Carl's staying behind with him the following morning. Accordingly at breakfast he said, "Well, Carl, it is going to be very lonely for me when you are all gone—and very hard for Mamma when Max is so sick, to take care of two little boys. What would you think of staying with me?" "And not go to the 'Merica?" he asked, with a look of unutterable disappointment in his face. "Not now, dear, but later when Papa can go, you could go with him. Without Mamma and Max it will be, oh, so lonely here. And not to have anybody—but—well, I suppose I could stand it. But with Mamma always seasick and with Max to care for, I dread for her to have the extra care of looking after your clothing, your baths, your food and all of those things. I fear it is going to be a very hard trip for her anyhow. What do you think, my boy?"

Choking and swallowing and with two big tears rolling down his cheeks, he looked up and said, "I think I had better stay with you, Papa. I will look after you." And so it was settled. No words can express how it touched his father's heart—or the tenderness that always existed between them after the experiences of that year together, cut off as they were from all other loved ones.

CHAPTER 14

SECOND RETURN TO AMERICA

When we went on board our Irrawaddy Flotilla Company's steamer en route for Rangoon we found a long rattan chair fitted up with cushions and rug and placed there for our comfort on the voyage by our good doctor. And what a comfort it proved to be! Max could lie in it, stretched out, all day on deck, and being light, it could easily be moved about to catch the breeze, making it so much more comfortable for him than having to be shut up in the hot cabin. He stood the trip down the river well but was, oh, so thin and weak. When we carried him on board our steamer in Rangoon he was as pitiful-looking a little object as one could possibly imagine. His fever had been so high that they had shaved his head of its mass of golden curls, his large blue eyes were sunken in their sockets, and he was so thin that he looked like a skeleton. When his father and Carl told us good-by and left the steamer, passengers turned away with tears in their eyes; for, as they told me afterwards, they felt perfectly sure that he had seen his father and brother for the last time, and that I would have to bury my little boy at sea within a week. But the doctor was right! The sea voyage was just what he needed. He began to gain immediately and within a week was walking a little about the deck. By the time we reached Marseilles little soft rings of gold had begun to cover his shaven head and he once more took on the appearance of a human being. It was interesting to watch his wonder and hear his questions as he came into a country of civilized life for the first time. What were those funny things on the houses? Meaning the chimneys. How did they paint all those flowers on the wall? He had never before seen wallpaper. When the maid at the hotel asked if the little boy would have cream on his porridge—"Mamma, what *is* cream?" he asked, much to the amusement of the maid. In the torrid plains of Burma little or no cream rises on the milk and the word was not in his vocabulary. The passengers to England talked much of the places they wanted to visit when they reached the homeland. There were English planters from Ceylon with their children and Government officers with theirs. All had been told of the wonders they would see when they reached the land of enchantment, England. One day I said, "Well, Max, my son, where do you want to go when we reach England?" "Well, Mamma," he said, "if I don't go anywhere else I want to go to the *Theological Garden* [Zoölogical Garden] and the—the—what is it, Mamma? the *Plaster Paris?*" [Crystal Palace.] You may be sure that he was taken to both of these places, at the former of which he had the joy of riding a dromedary and an elephant and of seeing the huge python, more than twenty-two feet long, which was caught by Dr. Vinton of Burma and presented through Sir Charles Bernard to the London Zoo.

On the trip across the Atlantic we encountered a storm. I had put Max to bed and gone to my dinner when the ship began to roll in a frightful way. Fearing my little boy would be thrown from his berth, I rushed back to my cabin. I shall never forget the look of terror on his face as I opened the door. He was grasping the side of his berth, his eyes were wide with fear and he said in a terrified voice, "Oh, Mamma, Mamma, the ship is going down — I *know* it is!" "Why, Max," I said, "who is it that takes care of us?" "Jesus," he said, in an almost inaudible voice. "Do you remember His ever having been in a storm at sea?" I asked. "Yes, Mamma, and He just said 'Peace—Be Still' and it all stopped, didn't it? And none of the 'sciples were drowned." "Well, do you not think He can take care of us just as well as He could of His other disciples? Just lie down and go to sleep—Jesus will take care of us," I said, and he was asleep in three minutes, though I braced myself and for hours it took all of my strength to keep him from being thrown from the berth. My muscles were lame for many days after. It was a terrible storm. The settees were wrenched from the deck and the compass was broken. Two ladies were thrown from their berths and severely injured. One lady went mad from terror and was obliged to return to

England by the same steamer as insane persons were not allowed to land in New York. I was told the next day after the storm that while I was quieting my little boy, panic prevailed among the passengers. Children cried and women screamed with terror, while both men and women called upon God for help. The first person upon his knees to cry for mercy was a diamond-bedecked prizefighter from Texas.

We had reached England in the heart of winter—January—and the damp penetrating cold after the torrid heat of Burma was most trying. I took a severe cold and traveling two or three days in dense fog my cold developed into a first-class case of pneumonia. The ship's doctor was very kind and attentive, but nevertheless I was a very sick woman when we reached New York, where I was met by Miss Newton, who was at the head of the Hospitality Committee. She had me taken at once to the home of Dr. Doukont, an efficient physician who had a "Prophet's Chamber" or Missionary's room where many a Missionary has been tenderly cared for and nursed back to life and health. In that room I stayed, receiving every possible care and comfort until able to travel on to my home in the Middle West.

The following year Mr. Carson and Carl came home. Being a very active and energetic man, nothing could be harder for Mr. Carson than doing nothing. Accordingly we took charge of the Kearney (Nebraska) Church during his furlough, and greatly enjoyed the work. The fellowship of Christians of our own kind was very precious and our people became greatly endeared to us.

At times the temptation to remain with them was strong. They loved us and we loved them. Then our little boys could not be taken back to the awful conditions that prevailed at that time in Burma. We were face to face with the supreme sacrifice in the Missionary's life—separation from children. *Could* we leave them? British officers and their wives did it for money. Could not we do it for Christ? When we thought of the unnumbered multitudes who did not even know that there was a plan of salvation from sin and of how much our years of experience would mean to the work, we felt that we could trust our precious boys, dearer to us than life itself, in God's hands with a perfect assurance that he would care for them. We placed them in the Home for Missionary's Children at Morgan Park, Illinois, just out of Chicago, and felt that they would have every possible care. We stayed there with them for a few days until they became a little acquainted, before setting out again for Burma.

PART 2

FOUNDING THE HAKA MISSION

CHAPTER 15

BEYOND THE PALE OF CIVILIZATION

We were summoned to meet the Board in Boston, where plans were discussed for opening up a new station in the heart of the Chin Hills, where no missionary work had ever been done by any denomination. It was the plan of the Board to form a chain of missions working both ways from the new station which we were to open up connecting with our lower Burma Missions in the Southeast and with those of Assam to the Northwest. My husband was greatly elated over this opportunity for he had long had the evangelization of these wholly neglected people on his heart.

We arrived in our old station of Thayetmyo, now in the hands of Mr. and Mrs. Baldwin, in the autumn of 1898. All of the Christians and school children were congregated on the bank of the river to welcome us. Our hearts were touched by our old Roman Catholic Tamil cook being among the first to greet us. He was competent and had a good place with a British officer who was paying him almost double what we could afford. He said to Mr. Carson: "I want to come back and work for you, sir." "But, Francis," Mr. Carson said to him, "though I would love to have you, we are going away up in the Chin Hills, where there are none of your people and I fear you would be very lonely." "No matter, sahib, I go wherever you go and I stay till I die," he said. Little any of us dreamed at the time how soon that would be. We were rejoiced to have our dear old servant back.

While I remained in the Thayetmyo mission visiting and helping as much as I could with the work Mr. Carson made a long tour of exploration up through the Chin Hills visiting all of the military posts and gathering all the information possible from the British officers in various places. The Superintendent of the Hills was most kind and courteous and helped in every way in providing information, but steadfastly refused to permit us to settle anywhere except where there was a British Post, saying that he would feel responsible for our safety and that he could not protect us elsewhere. Mr. Carson therefore decided upon Haka as the best place to establish our Mission, and put in an application to the Government for the beautiful thirty acres of land which now holds our Mission plant.

I think I cannot do better than insert here the description of the trip from Thayetmyo to Haka, written at the time and printed a few months later in the Missionary Magazine.

OPENING A FRONTIER STATION

On February 2, 1899, we left Thayetmyo, the scene of nine years of our missionary effort, with all our earthly possessions, en route for the Chin Hills, there to open work among a large tribe of Chins for whom, as yet, no mission work had ever been done. In order to save to the Union the expensive trip by regular passenger steamer we embarked on a cargo boat, the "Karanee." This steamer towed two flats, one on either side, each of which was loaded with ngapi (putrid fish) which is largely used as food by the people of this country. The night was hot and the fumes from the fish made me very sick all night so that I could not sleep.

Our cabin was so crowded that we had to slide one of the cotbeds out of the door in the morning in order to have standing room for dressing. Even then we had to dress one at a time. We were glad to get on the upper deck in the morning, where we found things clean and comfortable and a little removed from the stifling, sickening, indescribable smell of the ngapi.

The scenery along the Irrawaddy is beautiful. We glided slowly along, passing many large Burman rowboats; also raft after raft of fine teak logs or bamboos lashed together, upon which were tiny grass huts in which live women and children for weeks together, as the rafts are being floated down the river in order to find a market for the logs and bamboos.

On account of innumerable shallows and sandbanks it is impossible to run at night, and our steamer dropped anchor the first night in midstream opposite Fort Minhla, where the British met the strongest resistance during the last Burmese war. In an idol house near the fort, more than twelve years ago, Mr. Thomas, my husband and I, held some rousing gospel meetings with the British soldiers then stationed in that place.

Our first stop the following day was at Minbu, where our mission has an outstation established by Mr. Tilbe years ago, where there are some Burman Christians greatly in need of a shepherd.

The steamer company's agent came on board, and I found him to be a young Anglo-Indian man who had been in my Sunday-school class in Bassein fifteen years ago. Sunday was a hot, quiet day. We anchored for the night at Yeanangyoung, where there are extensive oil wells, owned by an English company, but operated entirely by Americans. These are, with two exceptions, I think, the only Americans in Burma, aside from the Baptist and Methodist missionaries.

Monday morning not a little excitement was created by a Burman canoe trying to cross our bows and very nearly being run over by the steamer. Fortunately the canoe caught on one of the fiats, and by the steamer's backing off, the man was saved. Nothing else of special note occurred during the long, hot day.

In the evening we stopped at Sale Myo and went on shore for a walk in this strange old place. The whole country round about looked bare and desolate, and one could but wonder where the people got the means of existence. The people seemed "thrifty" and well-to-do, however, and we learned that most of them are engaged in weaving, by hand, cotton blankets which they sell to passengers on the steamers. Women came aboard our boat with great bundles of them on their heads and many good bargains were made.

On the 7th we passed the old capital, Pagan. Formerly, it was a large and influential city; but now it looks comparatively deserted and in ruins. It is built on bare, rugged hills overlooking the river and pagodas are everywhere—thick almost as shocks of grain in an oat field after a bountiful harvest! As we stood on an eminence overlooking a broad stretch of country, we could have counted hundreds of them. Indeed, the people say that they have nine hundred and ninety-nine, but they cannot have a thousand because every time they build a new one, before it is completed an old one tumbles down! After leaving Pagan our next stop was at Pakokku—the end of our journey by the Irrawaddy River. We found we must wait three days before we could get a steamer up the Chindwin River.

We were not far from Myingyan, the home of our faithful missionaries, the Cases, so we took passage on the daily ferry and went to spend our waiting time with them. We arrived at the landing-place at four o'clock P.M. The heat was intense. We climbed up a very high, almost perpendicular bank of pure sand, after which, with the perspiration making roads through the dust and sand on my face, I was helped into the back of a two-wheeled oxcart, where I was protected somewhat from the fierce rays of the sun by a bamboo mat fastened over the cart in the shape of a woman's old-fashioned shaker bonnet—my umbrella doing service as the crown. For over two miles, sitting flat on the bottom of the cart, I rode through dust, without any exaggeration, a foot deep. Sometimes the wind would swirl it inside our "shaker" until it would almost suffocate us. My husband and Mr. Case walked, or rather waded, through the dust, except where we had to cross some large mud-holes, when they too clambered into the cart. Very dusty and warm, and very much cramped from sitting so long, flat on the bottom of the cart, we finally reached the house, where we were cordially welcomed by Mrs. Case and the boys, and where we had a delightful visit. The following morning, taking the little organ and our hymn books and Bibles, we all went under some fine old trees near the bazaar and commenced singing. It was "big bazaar day," and soon we were surrounded by a large crowd of people to whom my husband and Mr. Case very earnestly proclaimed the words of life.

Very attentively and respectfully the people listened—to what purpose God knows.

On the morning of the 11th we started back to Pakokku, leaving the house just at dawn. In the freshness of the morning, with the "shaker" top removed from the cart, the ride, notwithstanding ruts and bumps and dust, was almost enjoyable. We took passage on a tiny launch, and arrived in Pakokku about noon. Next morning, aboard a small stern-wheel steamer, we started up the Chindwm River. In the afternoon we met with a terrible Wind and sand Storm. In vain the captain tried to make way against it. We made no progress, and finally we had to drop anchor, both at the prow and astern, to keep from being driven upon the sands. The captain told me afterwards that he greatly feared the steamer would be blown over on her side, as the water was shallow and the steamer not drawing many inches of water. At ten o'clock the next day we arrived at Monywa where I saw the last white woman I have seen for more than four months, The following day we passed some very beautiful scenery, and the captain very kindly asked us on the bridge that we might the better enjoy it. The great cliffs were most picturesque, and the trees were alive with monkeys—some little gray fellows and some large and black with white throats, We anchored in the evening at Okma, and went up the steep sandbanks into a large village, but we were so beset by hundreds of howling pariah dogs, and surrounded by vicious-looking buffaloes, that I was glad to return to the safety of the steamer, where I amused myself by watching scantily-clad Burman women carrying great loads of cordwood on their heads, down the steep bank, for the fueling of our steamer.

The next day we stopped at two places to allow the people to come on board to barter with the Burman traders, who had rented portions of the deck for their goods, and had come all the way from Pakokku for the purpose. For the half-hour the steamer stopped it was a veritable bedlam. Crowds of people jammed and pushed and jostled each other in their mad haste to make their purchases before the steamer should leave. There was a large trade in tobacco, betel, onions, garlic, parched beans, dried fish and ngapi.

On the 16th we arrived in Kalewa, and took our things to an empty bamboo bungalow where we remained until the 21st, working hard repacking and weighing our goods, and sewing them up in bagging, into sixty-pound loads, so that they could be carried by coolies up the mountains. On Sunday we had a prayer meeting with our native helpers. Four prayers were offered, each in a different language. On our last day at this place, an English officer came in from the district and came to have dinner with us. A clean but much worn sheet was improvised for a tablecloth, and with three-tined forks and iron plates we dined our English guest in fine style!

On the morning of the 21st we packed our things, with infinite difficulty, into four Burman rowboats, and with three men to each boat, we finally got started up the narrow tortuous stream, to be taken each day farther and farther from civilization. Going upstream our boats were propelled by means of bamboo poles. One man on either side, standing at the prow, would place one end of the bamboo firmly in the bottom of the stream, and the other against his bare shoulder; then bending his body almost double with the effort, he would run the whole length of the boat, pushing with all his might, thus slowly driving the boat forward against the swiftly flowing current. This poling is so hard that great callous lumps, as large as one's double fist, form on the shoulders of regular boatmen. Packed into as small space as we could possibly occupy, with a bamboo mat bent like the cover of an emigrant wagon to protect us from the sun, we proceeded on our way until late in the afternoon. As our boatmen got hot and tired some of them discarded every vestige of clothing—which seemed to us meager enough to begin with! Finally we reached rapids in the stream where everything had to be unloaded from the boats and carried for half a mile upstream, the boatmen finding it all they could do to work the empty boats, one at a time through the rapids. It was night by the time we got all our things beyond the rapids, so we cooked our dinners over little camp fires, here and there on the sand, and ate them in the bright moonlight with our plates in our laps. We spread some quilts on the "corduroy" floor of a little grass hut and slept as best we could until about five o'clock in the morning, when we were up and soon on our way. During the day we several times encountered shallows where the boatmen, stripped of clothing, jumped into the stream and by desperate pulling and pushing worked the boats into deeper water. Once a boatman, when poling where the water was quite deep, slipped and tumbled headlong into the stream. He smiled grimly when asked if that was the way he always took a bath. Long after dark we reached Kalemyo, and after great difficulty found the landing opposite a bungalow built by the English Government for the accommodation of officers on tour.

We took possession for the night, for it contained bedstead, chairs and table, and we were able to make ourselves quite comfortable. Next morning we received a message from the superintendent of the Chin Hills, telling us to discontinue our journey by boat, as the water had fallen above and we would not be able to proceed with boats more than a short distance above where we were. He said he was sending ten pack mules to help with our goods, and would send as many coolies as we wanted. We found an English officer in the town who was looking after the rationing of the Sepoys stationed in the Chin Hills. He also advised us to dismiss our boats, telling us he could furnish us with pack cattle, so that we need not wait for coolies to come down from Falam.

As nothing can be taken into the Hills during the six months of rain, and as little necessary to the existence and comfort of an European can be had there, we had not only the furniture for our own house, but provisions of all kinds for six months, for ourselves and for the five native helpers who accompanied us. So, as one bullock or mule is supposed to carry only one hundred and twenty pounds and a coolie sixty pounds, the question of transportation was rather a momentous one. We sent word to the superintendent that we were coming with pack cattle and to send only a few coolies to carry dishes, lamps and such things as we dare not trust to pack cattle. The owner of the pack cattle came around to load up our goods; but after looking at them he decided that there were only a few of the smallest and most unimportant of the loads that he could take on his cattle; besides, his charges were so exorbitant that employing him was quite out of the question. With very heavy hearts we sent him away, not knowing what to do. The rationing officer had, to his great delight, obtained the use of an elephant and gone off on a tiger hunt, so we were unable to get any assistance from him. We found it impossible to get food for love or money; we also found it impossible to procure transport of any kind to go into the Hills. We succeeded in buying a few potatoes about the size and shape of marbles, from some Chins who had brought them down from the Hills to trade for tobacco. We dined that night and breakfasted next morning on potato curry. In the evening, while going through the bazaar in the vain search for something to eat, we noticed an old man sitting in front of his shop reading a book which looked like a Burmese Bible. We approached and asked what book he was reading. Sure enough, it was a Bible, and he was a Christian! We were mutually surprised and delighted—for he had no more expected to see missionaries there than we had hoped to find a Christian. We soon enlisted his services in trying to obtain food for us. He promised to bring rice, eggs and chickens the next day.

The superintendent at Falam was out of the station and we could not reach him with a message. At least message after message was sent to him for transport coolies, but brought us no response. Finally we heliographed the Subhadar Major of the Sepoys there, and after long waiting received a reply that the coolies would be sent in due time. They must first be collected from the different villages, which would require some time, and it would take at least three days for them to reach us after they were collected. We tried to "possess our souls in patience." The next day, according to promise, the old Christian came bringing what *had been* a dozen eggs. These he had tied up in his handkerchief and had had the misfortune to let them fall, breaking all but three or four. With a most woebegone look he approached us, with the chicken under one arm and in his hand carrying the eggs dripping through the dirty handkerchief. Nevertheless, he was a most welcome sight to our hungry eyes. He persistently refused to receive any compensation for these things, though we learned he had walked two miles through the blistering sun to another village to procure them for us. One, two more days passed and still no news of coolies. Sunday came and with it the old Christian and quite a number of heathen, to whom my husband preached and explained the Way of Salvation. In the evening two English government officers came in from a long trip on tour. We were obliged to share the house with them; they were tired and hungry; I knew I ought to ask them to dinner, but what was I to give them? Half of the chicken which we had kept for Sunday still remained, but "what was that among so many?" That very morning I had read, during our Bible study, "given to hospitality"—and so I decided to ask them, and do the best I could. The Lord provided that dinner! After we had asked them, and they had eagerly accepted, and I was cudgeling my brain to know how to make the best of the little I had, the servants of the officers came in bringing a fine large deer, a generous piece of which was immediately sent to us. This made a delicious soup and a fine roast, and I am sure to those tired, hungry men that dinner was a success! They left early next morning. All that night and the next day my husband had fever. I shall never forget the anxiety of that day. In a place where no food except rice was to be had at any price, my husband ill and no help accessible from any civilized human being, and so far as I could see, no hope of ever getting away, the outlook indeed seemed dark, but toward evening my husband's fever passed off, the rationing officer returned, and things began to brighten. We decided to start next morning in government boats, which were placed at our disposal, two days' journey farther up the stream, to a village where we would be able to get food and there await our coolies. After coming to this decision we went to bed with lighter hearts; but when morning came we found it impossible to get boatmen in time to get our goods off that day, so there was another day of weary waiting.

Next morning at half past ten, after endless vexations, we got the boats started. We, ourselves, had been invited by the officer to have breakfast with him, and in the afternoon, on a pony which he would provide, and a mule which had been sent down for me, we were to ride up and overtake our boats where they would anchor for the night. At four o'clock, I on a gay and festive government mule, and my husband on a sleek little pony, we started on our nine-mile ride. We found that we must cross the river on a raft. This raft was made by placing a platform with a railing around it across two long, narrow boats. With a deal of trouble we succeeded in getting our animals and ourselves on board, and crossing the deepest of the water; but long before we neared the farther bank we found the water so shallow that we could proceed no further with our raft. The mule did not enjoy the idea of getting out into the water and we had a terrible time with her. When finally we did succeed in getting her off, I feared we should never get her to stand close enough to the raft for me to mount. After vainly persuading her for a long time and being nearly jerked off into the water several times, I made a desperate leap and fortunately landed across the saddle—the mule starting on through the water without waiting for me to adjust myself. I barely had time to put myself to rights before we came to a very high bank almost perpendicular, up which we had to climb. After gaining the top of the bank we rode for miles through dense elephant, or *kine*, grass fifteen or twenty feet high, which towered high above our heads. We knew that this grass made an excellent place for tigers to hide, and that there were many in the vicinity. I, at least, kept a keen lookout, but was not rewarded with the sight of a tiger. After a time our path broadened and we came out into a beautiful bamboo jungle; the graceful, willowy trees met in arches over our heads; now and again we startled jungle fowl which seemed but little frightened at our approach. We saw squirrels leaping about in the trees, heard a "barking" deer in the distance, and pheasants drumming in the forest. Once a huge wildcat scurried across the road in front of us. On we rode through two small clearings where there were rice fields and villages, and finally, just at dark, we rode up to the zayat, the place our boats were anchored.

The zayat consisted of a very rough floor, high off the ground, with a roof over it. The wind was sweeping a perfect gale through it. To get up on the floor we had to climb a notched pole, in lieu of a ladder, which proved for the stout member of our party rather a difficult feat! However, it was accomplished, and there with our plates in our laps, and the wind fairly tearing the hair from our heads, we ate our dinner, after which we spread some quilts on the floor and tried to sleep—but with indifferent success. Next morning we were up and off in our boats before daylight. We anchored about 10:30 by a broad sandbank, where our breakfasts were cooked and eaten. Each set of boatmen and our own people were squatted here and there around separate fires, and soon ricepots were steaming in every direction.

After a hearty breakfast and a good rest for the boatmen, we proceeded very comfortably, for the day was cloudy and cool. We reached Indin, the end of our journey by boat, about 4:30, and here also we occupied a government bungalow. We settled down to wait as patiently as possible the coming of our coolies. Here at least we could get food. Fortunately we stored all of our goods under the house, for in the night there came up a terrible storm. Furies were in the wind, and the rain came down in torrents. We feared all of our goods would be ruined, but nothing was seriously injured. Here we again unpacked and repacked, throwing out all broken dishes, etc., which were not a few, and putting everything in the smallest possible compass. On the eve of March 6th our coolies arrived. My heart almost quailed when I thought of trusting ourselves and all that we had to the hands of such fierce, savage-looking creatures. They were carrying spears and guns, they were almost naked and their bodies were encrusted with filth which had been accumulating for years. We could not speak one word that they could understand; nevertheless, we got off next morning with less trouble than we had anticipated. We were indeed a motley crew as we wended our way up the mountains, but, oh, how glad we were to get started! First came the coolies with their promiscuous loads of boxes, barrels, beds, chairs, etc. Next came the only white male member of our party, on foot, with a gun on his shoulder and carrying a canteen of water. Next came a stout white woman mounted on a yellow mule, followed by two mounted Sepoy guards sent for our protection by the Superintendent of the Hills. Next came a Karen preacher, an Indian cook with his Burmese wife, and two Christian Chin girls. Bringing up the rear were ten tiny sore-backed pack mules driven by two Chinamen.

We marched up the narrow mountain path, a gradual ascent for eight miles, when we stopped at a rest-house by a beautiful mountain stream. We had started before breakfast thinking to get to this place in time to have breakfast about half-past ten or eleven o'clock, but our coolies were in no hurry and did not arrive with the things until two o'clock. We breakfasted at two forty-five. After an eight-mile ride, all the way up hill, we were quite ready for our breakfast by the time we got it. We were up next morning at four o'clock and this time had breakfast before we started. We got off just at daybreak and traveled thirteen miles, up one mountain side and down another, sometimes on steep mountain sides by narrow footpaths, with clear mountain streams dashing in rapids and cascades hundreds of feet below. This march, though very wearying, was most interesting.

We passed through pine forests—the first pines I had seen in the country. Sparkling springs leaped from shady hillsides where the banks were covered with loveliest ferns. Blue and yellow Convolvulus smiled at us from every turn in the road, and stately Rhododendrons bowed their flaming flower-crowned heads at us as we passed. Monkeys screamed and chattered in the trees. We camped in a little pine bungalow beside a dashing mountain stream. In the evening our Chin coolies favored us with a concert, and I found they were using my bandbox, which contained all the millinery I possessed in the world, for *a drum!* They had carried the box during the day, and seemed delighted that they had discovered its use.

We were up in the morning and off again at daybreak. Up, up, up! The road was so steep that I sat doubled up in my saddle and was so cramped that I could hardly endure it.

We encountered a fierce mountain storm. The wind lashed the trees, which swayed and creaked until I was in an agony of fear lest they should break and crash down upon us. Presently a cold rain came on and pelted us in our faces until we could hardly see the road. We were drenched to the skin. Twice we met trains of pack cattle on the narrow shelf of a mountain side. The path was so narrow that we had to hug the side of the mountain, standing perfectly still until the cattle got by, rubbing against us as they passed. I hardly know which I feared the more, being crowded over the precipice or being crushed by the passing animals.

When we reached camp we were wet and cold and had to wait for hours for our coolies to come with dry-clothing and food. At this camp we met an English lieutenant on his way to England on sick leave. He had been affected by exposure to the sun, and was partially paralyzed. He was the first white man we had seen since leaving Indin. The following day our journey was a gradual descent. I walked five miles in the morning and enjoyed it; but when, towards the end of our march my mule's back got sore so I had to get down and walk another mile and a half, I found myself so stiff and lame that dragging myself into camp was anything but pleasure. On this march we passed many wild peach trees loaded with blossoms. We camped near a suspension bridge built by the English Government across the Manipur River, which flowed through a great mountain gulch.

After the coolies came up with our goods we showed them the sewing machine, concerning the use of which they had speculated a good deal. They had never seen a piece of machinery before and were greatly interested and delighted. Some of them were women, their only dress being skirts not more than eighteen inches long, and huge brass hairpins, thrust through knots of thick black hair at the nape of the neck. Some of these hairpins actually weigh as much as five pounds each! I gave each of the women a needle and a safety-pin, after explaining their use. They were perfectly delighted. They patted my cheek and stroked my shoulder (a Chin method of showing gratitude and affection) and some of them even came up and put their arms around me.

The following day we had an abrupt ascent, steeper than anything preceding. We got so high, the side of the mountain was so steep and the path so narrow, that I grew dizzy and dared not for a moment look down. "Underneath are the everlasting arms" was my constant comfort. After a long and weary march we reached Falam, a military post, and the home of the Superintendent of the Hills, in whose house we put up over Sunday, and who showed us many kindnesses.

After a good rest and good food we were greatly refreshed and made the three days' journey from Falam to Haka with comparative comfort.

We arrived in Haka March 15, six weeks after setting out from Thayetmyo. We rented a little two-roomed house of Government and soon had our things in it and were settled down for work.

Haka is situated on the side of a great mountain. It is a military post where are stationed sixty Sepoys with three English officers. Chin villages abound on the neighboring hillsides. Many thousands of people are accessible from this place, not one of whom is a Christian and not one can read and write in any language. Their only religion is the sacrificing of animals to evil spirits; it is also their only system of medicine. To these poor people we hope to introduce the elevating, uplifting influence of the gospel of Christ and teach them the Way of Salvation.

CHAPTER 16

LOVING THE UNLOVELY

Should I live to be a hundred years old I shall never forget the experiences of our first night in Haka. I had comforted myself on the way with the thought that our coolies were the lowest class of people and that when we reached Haka and the higher classes we would find them cleaner and far less repulsive in appearance. The news had gone ahead of us that a white man was coming and bringing his wife. They had never seen a white woman, and people flocked in from all the neighboring villages *to see the elephant!* I was on exhibition for weeks! People from all over the Hills came to see me. I had one gold-encased tooth holding a bridge. They had never seen anything of the kind and evidently it was an object of great speculation and interest to them, for one of their first requests to me was this: "Will the Boinu open her mouth and let us see her *brass* tooth?"

But as the crowds flocked about us on the evening of our arrival, I looked about in vain for the cleaner, less repulsive, higher-class people. My heart sank, for I could not tell the chiefs from the coolies. *All* were dirty and filthy beyond description. A British Assistant Superintendent of the Hills was stationed at Haka, but he had been absent for more than two months. He had heard we were coming and sent a kind note of welcome and told us to go into his house and make ourselves as comfortable as we could until we could make other arrangements.

At Falam the Superintendent had not only furnished his house cozily and comfortably, but he had sent to England for flower seeds and had all of the sweet home flowers—which do not grow in the hot Burma plains—blossoming in profusion in the yard. I was delighted, and had visions of something similar upon our arrival in Haka. But the Assistant Superintendent having been absent so long, the whole station was overgrown with weeds and not one single flower was in evidence. When we entered his little two-roomed stone and mud hut, with no floor and the ground under our feet worn into hills and valleys, we found in the way of furniture only a small rickety pine table and a canvas deck chair—nothing more. Neither of us said a word for a long time. My husband *felt* my disappointment. Our things were brought in and I began spreading the quilts on the bumpy dirt floor for our bed. Finally, sitting there Turk fashion on the hard ground, I broke out with, "Arthur, I can't do it! I simply *can't* do it!"

"Can't do what?" he asked, his voice full of sympathy. "I can't stand it to shut ourselves out from the world and shut ourselves in with such people as these and in a place like this and never see or know anything else. I thought I could go with you anywhere that God called and stay there and work with you. But I have been weighed in the balance and found wanting. Oh, Arthur, I can't—I *can't* stay on and live out my life in this awful place, among these loathsome people." And I wept bitterly not more because of my disappointment in the place and the people than for my own inability to meet the situation bravely. "Never mind," my husband said. "Don't think any more about it to-night. Just try to go to sleep. You don't have to stay here if you don't want to. There are plenty of other places to work and we can go back to the plains. I never dreamed you would feel like this. But just go to sleep with the thought that you do not have to stay—unless you want to. I would not keep you up here for the world and have you feel like this," he said very tenderly. "Weighed in the balance and found wanting," I sobbed out again in a heart-breaking, despairing wail.

The next morning we got up early and looked about us. Our coolies came to be paid off. Some were women and some were men. One girl about eighteen was unusually attractive. I had tried, though we knew not a word in common, to make friends with her on the way up the Hills. Her perfect figure was clad in a skirt not more than eighteen inches long—that was all. With a beaming face she came to say good-by, patting my face with a very grimy hand and smiling into my eyes. As I looked into her bright face I realized that Drummond was right when he said, "Love is the greatest thing in the world." It is. I saw beyond the grime and filth on that perfectly formed and almost nude body. I saw the need of the soul. I saw the possibilities of that fresh, young life, and thousands more like her. What could not a consecrated Christian woman do for her and those of her kind if she would? What a matchless opportunity had been given me! What more could one ask for than to spend her life striving to better the conditions of such as she? Turn away from a people because they were the most needy of any I had ever seen? Go back to the plains? God forbid! "You coward, you coward," I said over and over again to myself.

In all my twenty-one years in those Hills I never had another really homesick day. Lonely ones there have been. For ten long months at a time I have not seen the face of another white woman and rarely any one to whom I could speak in my own tongue. The *days* were not really lonely either. They were too full with school work, medical work, entertaining native visitors and translation work, to leave any time for loneliness. It was the evenings when superstitions keep the native people from going out, evenings when the rain was pouring down in torrents and everything was damp, chilly and moldy, evenings when you knew none of your kind was within days' travel of you—such evenings it was that sometimes became unbearable and drove one almost to madness.

CHAPTER 17

WORKING UNDER DIFFICULTIES

We rented from the Government (British) a little two-roomed stone and mud house, without any floor, very similar to the one so kindly placed at our disposal by the Assistant Superintendent upon our arrival. With the furniture which we brought with us we made ourselves fairly comfortable and immediately began work. Obviously the first things to do were to get a place of our own and to learn the language of our people.

We found it difficult to get a teacher. The people were suspicious of us. Before the English occupation of their Hills they had been wont to raid the Burman villages of the foothills and carry away the children as slaves. They told us long afterwards that they believed we were placed there by the Government (British) to somehow work up some secret scheme to get hold of *their* children and send them to the British for slaves. They could not believe it possible that we were there solely for their good.

We finally succeeded in hiring a man to come and talk to us for two or three hours every day in order that we might get some insight into the language. We had not one thing to help us, not even an alphabet, for the language was not yet reduced to writing. It was an uphill job. We soon learned to get nouns without difficulty, and wrote one down as soon as we were sure of it. But verbs! When we wanted such verbs as to drink, to run, to eat, we could usually succeed by giving a demonstration. But consider the difficulty in getting such words as to learn, to love, to worship, to act, etc.

Imagine one's chagrin when after wrinkling his forehead, scratching his head, and looking wise trying to get the word to think, he finds when he comes to use it, he has the word to scratch; or when he wants the word to perspire he gets to rain; or when he thinks he is saying, "Come and eat" he really says, "Come and chew." Then another difficulty was that the idea itself was so often wanting. My husband was trying to get the word to forgive. He said to the leading chief, "Shwe Lien, your brother Koke Hnin and Tat Hmone are great friends; supposing they should quarrel and both become very angry and Tat Hmone should bite off Koke Hnin's ear—a not unusual performance between Chin men when exasperated beyond endurance—and afterwards he would be very sorry he had done it and would go to Koke Hnin and say how sorry he was and he wanted him to forget what had happened—wanted their friendship to be as before—what word would he use?" "We would not need any word for that, Boipa, *for we would never do it*," replied the old chief.

It was several months before we got the Government's sanction to our application for land for our mission compound. But at last it came, a grant of thirty acres of the most beautiful land in the vicinity. One big chief, Lien Mo, had a claim on part of it, which we bought for forty-five rupees. Though it was covered with pine forest this was all he asked, and all that our beautiful compound cost. The next thing was to build a house. But how was this to be done? There was not a brick nor a board to be had. Mr. Carson succeeded in borrowing some Goorkha sawyers from the Government. He hired Chins to cut down trees on the mountain sides which these sawyers converted by hand into boards and timbers for building. They were carried on men's shoulders for miles to the mission site.

Five times the wage received in the plains was offered carpenters to come up to do the building; but nothing would induce them. Neither, at that time, could Chinese carpenters be persuaded to come. All were afraid of the wild, savage Chins who, until stopped by their British conquerors, decorated their houses with human skulls.

In speaking of his failure to get carpenters, Mr. Carson said, "Well, I know what I can do. I can build the house myself." "How can you build it?" I said. "You're not a carpenter." "No, but a man can do anything that he has to," he said, "and you know my motto—'I can do all things through Christ, who strengtheneth me.'" And he did build it. First there must be bricks for foundation and chimneys. He searched until he found clay that would make bricks. Then he made molds and molded, dried and burned the bricks. Now there must be mortar to hold them together. He searched until he found sandstone. This he hired pounded and sifted and carried in bags to the place of building. Limestone he also found and taught a man to burn it. This also was carried in on men's backs. Every brick he laid himself. Every board and timber was sawed and planed and put into place by his own hands. Sashes, doors and steel roofing were ordered from America; beaver board, for ceiling and partitions, from England; the paint was from Germany, the glass from China, and the furnishings from India. Who shall say it was not a cosmopolitan house? Was any house ever erected more loved and appreciated, I wonder. When we told the natives about Heaven they would ask if it were nicer than our house.

But long before this house was completed, I was obliged to return to America—to make other arrangements for our children. That sentence may not seem to mean much, but it involved days of mental agony, nights of planning, praying and suffering. It meant leaving my husband alone with those wild, uncivilized people for years.

The faithful family servant who had said he would go anywhere with his master and stay till he died had literally done so. Only two months after reaching Haka he died very suddenly, the altitude proving too high for his heart. Besides feeling his loss very keenly, his death left us in desperate straits for a servant. We had no stove; it was the rainy season and we had difficulty in getting wood that was dry enough to burn. I would go out to our little cookhouse and try to cook over an open fire with wet wood. The smoke would nearly put my eyes out. My husband would send me into the house and try his hand at it—and succeed better. But it was uphill work and interfered with other things we wished to do.

Sympathetic officers in Falam sent us an old Indian man to try. Though he spoke no English and was untrained they hoped he would be some help. His name was Anthony, but my husband called him Anti—"Short for Antifat"—which is significant. Finally a kind officer loaned us his cook to train a Chin. We found one willing and teachable and with my help soon got on nicely, but it was hard for Mr. Carson to be left with poorly trained Chin service and without the companionship and efficient help of his devoted Francis who had so delighted in serving him.

For Mr. Carson, my going home meant study of the language, translation work, school work, evangelistic work, and medical work to say nothing of mason and carpenter work. All this without one sympathizing heart to help him. The country was still very unsettled which made it much harder for me to leave him alone. Only a short time before we knew this separation must come there had been an insurrection.

The Chins had been getting hold of so many guns that the British who had only been administering the Hills for a short time feared there might be trouble and ordered all guns brought in and registered and only a certain small number, according to the population of the various villages, returned to the Chins.

One day while all British officers of the three "Posts"—Falam, Tiddim and Haka—were collecting these guns, the leading chief, who spoke Burmese fairly well and with whom my husband had made friends, came in looking greatly excited and shut the door.

Standing with his back against it, he asked if there was any one else in the house besides ourselves. When assured there was not he said that he had something very important to tell us; that no one must ever know that he had told or it would cost him his head.

He shook with excitement as he told us that the people did not propose to give up their guns. He said Chins loved their guns better than anything else in the world; that it would be easier to give up wives and children, because they could get plenty more wives and children, but couldn't get guns!

He said that the chiefs had "eaten mud" (taken the sacred oath by mingling their blood, taken from their legs, with earth and eating it) that they would not relinquish their guns but would kill off the British officers, take their guns, and take back the administration of their own Hills.

All were to be killed except the Superintendent who was to be held for ransom in order to make terms with the Government.

Shwe Lien said, "You are my friends, you have been kind to me, I do not want you to be killed. That is why I have risked my life to tell you that to-night Chins all over the Hills will rise up and kill off the white people and sepoys. None of my people will kill you. I will stand by your side, and if you die I will die first. Don't be afraid, you have been my friends. But don't let any one know that I have been here to warn you," and with this he was gone.

We looked blankly at each other, wondering just how much it meant. Then we began discussing plans to protect ourselves and the three Christians who were with us.

An hour or two later we received a heliograph message from the Superintendent, who was on tour, telling us that he had just received authentic information that there was to be an uprising that night and that all white people were to be killed. He advised us to take any valuable papers and money that we might have and go into the police lines for protection.

He told my husband to consult with the Havildar, (sepoy officer) telling him everything and with his assistance to make ourselves as secure as possible. He said he would have a British officer on the spot at the earliest possible moment.

We decided we could protect ourselves better in our own house than in the police lines and the guards were arranged accordingly.

My husband had presented me with a beautiful little rifle which he had purposely taught me to use in the presence of the people, feeling that my having a rifle and knowing how to use it would be a protection to me when he was absent, as was often necessary. That night he oiled and cleaned both rifles, putting them in perfect condition. Handing mine to me, he said, "Now, Laura, you must be prepared to use this to-night."

"Why, Arthur," I said, "I would rather die than shoot anybody!"

"If they shoot at us, or enter our house with swords and knives and threaten us, you must shoot, and shoot to hit—but aim at their feet. Of course, we would not shoot to kill," he replied.

We lay down, fully dressed, each with a hand on a rifle. But morning came and there was no disturbance. However, it was not all a farce. Just before the Superintendent had sent the heliograph message to us a faithful Chin servant, who loved his master, revealed the plot to him much as Shwe Lien had revealed it to us.

The plan was to attack the Superintendent's camp first and thus frighten others into easy submission. Being forewarned, the Superintendent was on the alert with his sepoys in readiness, and just as the Chins were ready to attack his camp the sepoys attacked them. They scattered in every direction. The sepoys pursued and took many captives. Another band of Chins attacked an Indian cow-keeper's village, killed some of the inhabitants and looted the village. A British officer came upon them as they were dividing the spoil. The leaders were captured. After trial, twelve of the ringleaders in the insurrection were transported and three were hanged. These drastic measures quieted things in the Hills for several years.

CHAPTER 18

EMERGENCY RETURN TO AMERICA

My passage was engaged for America and arrangements were made for me to take three children of other missionaries who must be sent home to school. These children were Carroll Roach and Mabel and Gladys Bushell. Shortly before time to leave Haka there came a terrible cloudburst which completely wrecked the suspension bridge over the Manipur River. The planks were all torn off and the cable on one side was broken. At that time of the year the only way to get down the mountains was by way of that bridge.

Government had two planks each about ten inches wide put side by side across the middle on the timbers below, which were mostly intact, in order that coolies might cross with the mails. Orders were given that only one person must attempt crossing at a time.

The bridge was suspended from towers high above the swiftly flowing, roaring and tumbling mountain stream. Walking on the narrow planks, unable to touch anything with the hands to steady oneself, one cable down so the bridge swayed and tilted with every step, even the thought of crossing was nerve-racking in the extreme.

A British major, upon hearing we were going to cross, exclaimed, "Why, Mrs. Carson, all the gold on the Klondike would not induce me to attempt it." But I was not after gold. I was going to my children, who needed me, and I assured my husband that I was not afraid. Why, coolies crossed frequently with bags of mail on their backs. Why should I fear? He cautioned me not to look down but to keep my eyes fixed on the opposite bank, then he bravely started out ahead. My heart stood still as I watched him balancing himself on the long swaying bridge over the tumbling waters far below. He reached the other side in safety and gayly waved to me. But the strain of seeing him cross had been so great that had he not been on the other shore I would surely have backed out. Summoning all my courage, I started tremblingly forth. Midway across, the roaring of the water was so furious I could not resist the temptation to glance down. It was my undoing. I could not take another step. I started to get down on my hands and knees. "Stop that! Get up, look straight at me and come here!" called my husband in a commanding voice. He had never before spoken to me in such a tone and—I did exactly what he told me to! But the nervous strain had been so great that when I reached him my strength was all gone and I dropped my head on his shoulder and we both sobbed.

We reached Rangoon in time for the steamer and with the three children in my care I sailed in company with Mrs. Tilbe and her four little ones via England for the homeland. With seven lively youngsters to care for and amuse we had little time to brood over leaving our husbands behind.

Upon our arrival in New York we were met by Dr. Rhodes and shown every possible kindness. Mrs. Tilbe was very sick on the day of our arrival, and that night got aboard her Pullman with her little flock and went straight through to her home in St. Louis. But I took my little girls to Newton Center, Massachusetts, and left them and Carroll with dear Mrs. West while I went up into Maine to visit another Missionary's children and report upon their condition. On my return I took Carroll and turned him over to his grandfather somewhere in Illinois, and then went on to my own little boys who at that time were with my sisters in Nebraska.

Going to Grand Island where our Baptist college is located, I rented and furnished a house, made a home for my boys and put them in the public school. My husband's mother at that time lived in Aurora (Nebraska). After going down and nursing her through a hard siege of pneumonia I brought her back with me and she afterwards made her home with us. Her little home in Aurora was sold and another one was bought in Grand Island, into which we moved and there lived for four years while Mr. Carson wrought on, alone, in the Chin Hills.

Mr. Carson's mother being more than willing to help with the work at home, I was enabled to engage in outside interests.

Dr. E. F. Jorden, well known in Baptist circles, was at that time pastor of the First Baptist Church at Grand Island, and I became his assistant. I also taught Biblical Literature two days a week at the College. Dr. George Sutherland was then President. To him and to Dr. Jorden I owe more than could ever be put into words for kindnesses and help through those hard, but in many ways, delightful years. No work that I have ever done in America I think has yielded me greater satisfaction and pleasure than that with my Bible class of college students and teachers, numbering above eighty, in the Grand Island Baptist Church. In later years, I have met them everywhere, leading such splendid purposeful lives that I am proud to have known them and to have been associated with them.

Upon Mr. Carson's return in 1903 we were immediately recalled to the Kearney Church, then in search of a pastor. It was a delight to be back with old friends among a people we loved, and an unspeakable joy to have a little home life with father, mother, sons, and grandmother all present. We remained with this church until our boys graduated from Kearney High School (in the same class), June, 1905. Their father preached the baccalaureate sermon.

That summer, after making arrangements for our boys to enter Grand Island College in the autumn, we spent with them making farewell visits among relatives and friends. When visiting my sister in Idaho she and her husband gave us what I recall as one of the greatest treats of my life. With a farm wagon for our camping outfit, an Idaho "white-top" (broad-seated spring wagon with white canvas cover) and two or three saddle ponies, they took us on an enchanting three-weeks' camping trip through Yellowstone Park. We then visited my mother, brothers and sister in Southern California, after which we did deputation work up and down the Pacific Coast visiting many churches in the interest of Missions in California, Washington, and Oregon. On September 16th we assisted in the farewell services of Mr. Rhodes, under appointment to Burma, at the Centralia, Washington, Church, where Rev. H. S. Black, a beloved old college chum of Mr. Carson's, was pastor. Here the following morning we knelt together and committed our dear boys to our Father's care before seeing them off for college. That was the last time the boys ever saw their almost idolized father.

On the 21st we sailed on the *S. S. Dakota* for Hongkong en route for Burma. We were delayed three weeks in Yokohama for the unloading and reloading of our steamer, which gave us an opportunity to see the work of some of our splendid missions in Japan and also to visit our old school friend and devoted fellow missionary, Miss Annie Buzzell, at Sendai.

While lying in port in Yokohama, President Taft and his party, including Miss Alice Roosevelt, Nicholas Longworth, Mary Ellen Foster, and others arrived from the Philippines. Mrs. Foster, appointed by President Roosevelt to study conditions of Filipino women and children, had separated from the party and was a very delightful fellow-passenger with us from Singapore to Rangoon on her world's tour of Missions.

We left Yokohama October 14th, called at Kobe, Nagasaki, Shanghai, and reached Hongkong on the 26th of November. From there we sailed on a French steamer for Singapore, where we were detained for ten days and where we were delightfully entertained in the American Methodist Mission. They took us across the Straits to visit the Sultan's palace in the capital of the little independent state of Jahore. We were shown through the palace and saw many interesting things including the golden throne and a wonderful massive dinner set in solid gold. We visited the Mosque, where the Sultan worships, and went also to see the tigers, which, we were told, the Sultan was interested in procuring for commercial purposes. One huge creature had just been captured and brought in from the jungle. He had banged his head with such force against the iron bars of his cage that it was bruised and bleeding. Going a little too near, he turned my blood cold by striking fiercely at me through the bars and coming within a hair's breadth of laying me low!

A few days later found us aboard a British India steamer bound for Rangoon, where we arrived in due time, bought, packed into 60-pound loads, and shipped stores enough to do us for a year, and were soon on our way up country. We left Rangoon on December 1st and reached Haka, December 23rd, having traveled by rail, by river steamer, by native rowboat, by pony and on foot. The Easts and the natives gave us a cordial welcome.

CHAPTER 19

A MEDICAL MISSIONARY FOR HAKA

Dr. H. H. Tilbe had relieved Mr. Carson for the first year of his furlough, during which time he prepared the little Grammar of the language still in use. Dr. E. H. East came out to Mr. Carson for medical work during the second year of my absence from Haka. He was large hearted, efficient and sympathetic and was rapidly winning a large place in the hearts of the people. But just two months after his arrival he was taken with appendicitis and it became necessary to get him away as it would be perilous for him to remain where an operation would be impossible. Mr. Carson therefore took our bed springs, cut them in two and made a comfortable stretcher, over which he fixed a canopy of waterproof canvas, as it was the heart of the rainy season, and hiring coolies to carry him, started on the lugubrious fourteen days' march through pouring rain down the mountains to the river. It would be hard to picture Mr. Carson's feelings as he saw Dr. East, who had brought him such cheer and help, start back so soon to America. And who can know the heartache as he turned his face once more to his little home in the hills where the loneliness would only be augmented because of the two months of companionship?

The next time these two men met was in Chicago. Mr. Carson was on his way home and Dr. East preparing to return to Haka. He took with him, this time, a splendid addition to the mission in the person of his fine young wife. And there was a third one to greet us upon our arrival for they had a darling baby boy.

During our absence in America, through Dr. East's efforts, two fine men and their wives at Tiddim had become Christians and been baptized—the first fruits of our work in the Chin Hills. One, Tuam Hang, was a remarkable man, heir to a tribal chieftainship. Recognizing the fact that as a Christian he could not lead his people in their heathen ceremonies, nor follow their drunken customs, he relinquished his right to the chieftainship which would have made him a rich man, and became—and still is—a humble preacher of the Gospel on the munificent salary of six dollars a month!

The following is a letter from a native Karen preacher telling Dr. East of the first convert in the Chin Hills.

July 25, 1904, Koset Village.

Sir:—

Your letter came to me and tell about the school which you spoke with Mr. Fowler. We little three here [meaning his family] were very glad. The time when we arrived here in Koset till this time, we try as well as we can for preaching, so that one man name Paung Shwin, his among three chiefs which you had been seeing, he believes Jesus can save him from his sin into life. He gave up all the bad things and come to us for worship God together every time with his wife and mother. He's very earnest in preach to other. Some men spoke to him and make him afraid, but he do not care what was the people said to him. As he knew more about Christ he preach more and more to other people. The time when you come to Koset he will [be] Baptist at once. As well as my master can, come soon.

Now we little here glad every time to preach. We hope our master and mamma and Sya San Win and his wife will glad with us in prayer. I cannot write English well; if I can write you will glad more than this.

One man name's Turn Harm; he is a chief among the three chiefs. Now he begin to believe Jesus. This night he come up to me for prayer God. Dear master, please remember for Turn Harm in your prayer. O my dear master if you arrive here this time, how you will be very glad for Christ.

As to school the people begin to build the school now. They got some post to the school place; in a few days I think school will finish. Some time I wrote about to stop school until the school [house] finish, and you tell I must stop; but I think in my heart it is better to learn every day so that I have school in my house.

Remember Paung Shwin and his household your prayer. As well as I can I try in write English. Please know what I mean as well as you can.

Your obedient servant,

SHWE ZAN.

Up to the time of our return not one among the Haka people had been baptized; but Shia Kaw, a boy working in the East home had, through their teaching, become convinced of the truth of Christianity and about the time of our arrival asked for baptism. He showed every evidence of true conversion and on January 1, 1906, Mr. Carson baptized him in the lovely little lake on the Mission Compound in the presence of a large company of interested people.

From this time on, the work made marked progress, Mr. Carson and Dr. East working together harmoniously and enthusiastically. We all lived together while Dr. East built the second Mission house. Although he was able by this time to get Chinese carpenters he met and overcame many difficulties. I remember that he decided to plaster the walls of his house and in order to get the necessary hair to make the plaster stick, he bought defective gunny (rationing) bags from the Military Police and chopped them up, thus making a very good substitute for hair.

While in America Dr. East had raised money for a hospital and this he also built, a good building with accommodations for twenty patients besides a nice operating room and office. While Dr. East gave his time to the building and medical work, Mr. Carson devoted himself to language work and evangelistic endeavor while I took charge of the school work.

We tried not only to educate and Christianize the people but put forth every effort to provide some means by which they would be able to support a higher civilization. Through the help and generosity of a British officer my husband got a fine pair of stock cattle shipped out from Scotland. Unfortunately one died en route. Dr. East, with better success, brought out a splendid pair of pigs, which has improved the breed and added materially to the wealth of the people. We found that one of the principal articles of food for the people was Indian corn and that the corn grown in the Hills was of a very small and inferior variety of the flint kind. While in America, therefore, Mr. Carson went to a first-class farmer and had him select seed corn of the choicest variety for us. This we shelled and put in Mason jars packed in barrels and took with us. We called the people and gave out a little to each family cautioning them to save the first year's crop for seed. This they did and now the good corn is practically universal all over the Hills and is a great blessing, furnishing them a many times larger yield to the acre than the old variety and a much better quality of corn. Finding wild peaches indigenous to the country, we got seeds of finest varieties from Illinois and California and have successfully raised very choice peaches, from which the Chins are getting starts. Many other things we have introduced in the same way, making life a little less hard not for the Christians only, but for all the people in the Hills.

For a long time our schools were uphill work. Children accustomed to roving the jungle at leisure with bows and arrows or pellets and slings found the confinement of school intolerable. After sitting on the floor for an hour or so with book or slate a boy could stand it no longer and would hop up and be off to his jungle haunts and we would probably not see him again for a week. The little girls were greatly handicapped in that each one who came to school had to carry a baby on her back. She would sit and sway back and forth to keep her baby quiet as she learned her lesson, every now and then having to jump up and run home to the mother that the baby might be fed.

But gradually conditions improved, we gained the good will of the people, more children were sent to school and more people became Christians as they learned more of the truth.

CHAPTER 20

TANG TSIN AND TSONG HKAM

An unusually promising young married man living more than fifty miles from Haka became an enthusiastic convert. I shall never forget the day he was baptized. With a glowing face he came to me to say good-by. "When I tell my people about Christ and how happy I am, I believe the whole village will become Christian," he said, and he started joyfully back with that hope in his heart. But the news that he had become a Christian got home ahead of him and he was promptly called before the chief to give an account of himself. "They tell me you are worshiping the foreign God. You cannot do that and live in this village," said the chief. "Oh, but let me tell you what a wonderful God he is—a God who loves us and helps us and saves us from our sin," begged Tang Tsin. "You need not tell me anything about this God, and you cannot worship Him and live in this village. You know that if you do our own gods will be angry, our crops will fail, our cattle will not reproduce, our children will die and all kinds of trouble will come upon us. You have either got to renounce this foreign religion or be driven from the village," reiterated the chief.

In vain Tang Tsin pleaded with him. When he saw that it was hopeless, he went to the highest British officer in the Hills and asked him if because he had accepted the Christian faith the chief, under British law, could expel him from the village. He said that if it concerned himself only it would not matter, but that he had a wife and two children of his own, two children of a dead brother and a mother to support. They were not yet Christians, he could not go away and leave them, and it would be the same in any village to which he might go and take them.

After talking to him awhile the Superintendent said, "Well, Tang Tsin, go back to your village and as long as you live in accordance with the teaching of the missionaries, doing nothing wrong to anger the people, the British Government will stand behind you. The chief cannot drive you out of your village simply because you worship the Christian God," and an order to this effect was sent to the chief.

Tang Tsin went home with a light heart and set himself to the task of winning his people. He went where there was sickness and death and trouble of all kinds trying to follow his Master in going about doing good.

But the wily chief had thought out a plan whereby he hoped to checkmate the British officer. The land is owned by the chiefs and is parceled out to families and passed down from father to son; a certain per cent of the crop always going to the chief. But, for any grave and sufficient reason, according to their custom, the chief with the approval of his elders can take the land back and give it to another. He therefore called Tang Tsin and told him that they had decided, unless he abandoned the worship of the foreign God, the land which he cultivated and which had been in the family for generations would be taken from him. Tang Tsin said that he was trying to do only good among the people and begged him to spare to his family the land of his fathers. The chief finally said in derision, "If you want land to cultivate you may farm the sacred field." Now, the "Sacred Field" is land dedicated to the evil spirits; and the people believed as much as they believed in their own existence that any one planting a seed in that sacred ground would drop dead on the spot.

"Do you mean that?" eagerly asked Tang Tsin, "Do you really mean that I may farm the sacred field?" "Yes," said the chief, "if you dare to, you may." The next morning found Tang Tsin, bright and early, digging up the sacred field. People stood about in open-mouthed wonder expecting every moment to see him die. But he didn't die. He is living yet and preaching the gospel to every one with whom he comes in contact.

At the end of the season he came over to the mission and told us about farming the sacred field. He said, "Why, my corn was more than twice as tall as theirs [the land was rich, never having been tilled] and my pumpkins were huge, while theirs were not bigger than my double fists. The people tell me secretly that my God is greater than theirs because He gives me so much better crops than they get." He said that many were coming to believe in the God he worshiped but dared not confess it because of the persecution.

He said he could not read very well and he wanted us to tell him exactly what the Bible taught—just the things he could do and the things he couldn't do so he would know how to order his life. We had him learn the Ten Commandments and the great commandments of the New Testament. The great truths of the plan of salvation he already knew. He went about to the neighboring villages and preached to all who would listen to him.

After a time a man named Tsong Hkam, in a near-by village, got up courage to publicly confess his faith in God.

His chief was greatly exercised over the matter and sent for the big tribal chief to decide what should be done with him. He came and Tsong Hkam was summoned before him. Knowing of Tang Tsin's case, he began in a very conciliatory way saying, "We don't want to have any trouble over this matter. We don't want to go up to the English Government about it; but you know if you worship the foreign God, all kinds of calamity will come upon our village. Just drop this foreign religion and I will give you thirty rupees." (About ten dollars.)

"But you do not understand," said Tsong Hkam. "I believe the Christian religion is true. I am a Christian and shall always be one." For some time the chief continued trying to bribe, offering more and more; but when he found it was useless he became angry and said: "I have never in my life humiliated myself as I have in dealing with you to-day. You will either take what I have offered and give up the worship of this foreign God or you will take the worst beating any man ever had." "Then I will take the beating," Tsong Hkam replied. "Bare your back," the chief commanded. Tsong Hkam threw off his blanket. "Put your hands on your knees," was the next order, and down went his hands to his knees.

Then the chief called up three brutal men armed with bamboos and told them to give him fifteen strokes each, and to lay them on hard. The first man finished his fiendish task and the second began when Tsong Hkam fell to the earth. Raising his hand, he said, "Wait a moment," and, lifting his eyes to heaven, he prayed. He asked for strength to bear the torture then added (like Stephen of old), "Count it not against them, Father, for they don't understand—they don't understand."

Then he said, resuming his position with his hands on his knees, "Come on, I am ready now. There is one to beat me still." Filled with superstitious awe, the old chief slunk away and no man dared to strike again.

Tang Tsin lifted the poor man up, helped him to his own home and washed his terribly bruised and bleeding back. For five days he was unable to walk. When he got better they decided the best thing for him to do was to go home and go quietly about his work and await developments. This he did; and going out in his field to work one morning, he was met by a delegation, and the spokesman said, "What are you doing here? Unless you are going to renounce the foreign religion, this is no longer your farm." "Then it is no longer my farm," said Tsong Hkam. He gathered a load of firewood and went home. As he threw down the wood in the yard, some more men came saying, "You need not be bringing wood here. This is no longer your home. The chief has already given it to another family. He has taken your wife for a slave, and unless you give up worshiping the foreign God you will have to be his slave, too." "Then I will be his slave," said Tsong Hkam, and he actually went and served him for several months. He was so obedient and faithful that he won the confidence of the chief.

As the time for the Association at Haka drew near Tsong Hkam went to the chief and said, "I have tried to do my work well. I have never asked for a day's leave. The Christians are going to have a big meeting at Haka and I very much want to go. Will you give me permission?" Permission was given, and when at the meetings a list of names of people applying for baptism and church membership was read the name of Tsong Hkam was on the list. When the question was asked if anybody knew any reason why he should not be received, Tang Tsin arose and very graphically told the story that I have told here, closing with this remark: "I think when a man has given up his farm, his home, his wife and his liberty for Christ's sake, he ought to be baptized and numbered with the Christians." We thought so, too! He was received and baptized and, needless to say, is now one of the staunchest Christians in all our hills.

His case was taken up to the Government by the missionaries and the chief, who ordered him beaten, was fined, and Tsong Hkam's property, liberty and wife were restored.

CHAPTER 21

MR. CARSON'S LAST TOUR

Mr. Carson translated the International Sunday School lessons every week. He also translated Mrs. Judson's catechism and forty-two hymns and a spelling book which were typewritten and mimeographed by Mrs. East.

Besides the translation work, Mr. Carson made long preaching tours on foot to the jungle villages. This work he dearly loved—carrying the Word of Life into the regions where it had never been heard. Coming home from one of these trips ill, we discovered that he had appendicitis. It became chronic. Dr. East strongly advised his going to America for an operation. But it was only two years since we returned from America and the expense of the trip would be great. Another one of our missionaries had been operated on for the same trouble in the hot climate of Rangoon with fatal results. What *ought* we to do? Mr. Carson was greatly opposed to returning to America just as the work was beginning to move forward with such splendid strides. He recovered from a severe attack in January and hoped with care that he might not have another one. Meantime the date for our Annual Association drew near. Mrs. East was in delicate health and the Doctor dared not leave her. It was imperative that a missionary be at the Association to direct the work as important questions were to be discussed. Dr. East thought that if he traveled slowly and was careful the trip would do Mr. Carson good. The English civil surgeon for the Hills was consulted and was of the same opinion.

Accordingly we started on a nine days' trip to a distant jungle village to attend the Association. But unforeseen and unexpected difficulties had to be met. In one place there was a landslide. The whole side of a shale mountain had slid down over the trail and was still sliding. This we crossed at our peril and with great difficulty. Further on as we crossed the ridge of the mountain we were struck by a hurricane. The natives who were with us dropped flat on the ground to keep from being blown over the ridge. We were forced to dismount and the ponies became frightened and unmanageable. When the fury of the wind had subsided a little we had to walk down a path for five miles which was so steep and stony that we had difficulty in getting the ponies to follow us. But at last we reached the village and were joyfully welcomed by the Christians.

The meetings were excellent and Mr. Carson presided at all of them. He was kept busy every day from daylight until far into the night. On the last day I saw that he was growing very weary. On that day the one hundredth convert in the Chin Hills was baptized.

That night after the meetings were over the old malady, from which he never recovered, returned with manifold severity. But God was merciful and permitted us to reach home before the end came. Those nine days' traveling beside the stretcher, were they not a thousand years? Scores and scores of people came out to meet us miles before we reached Haka. Dr. Tilbe, Mr. Carson's closest, best-loved friend since college days, made forced marches and was with us at the last. Dr. East did everything that love and skill could suggest. But on April 1st, 1908, the great heart was stilled and I was alone. *Alone!*

Even after the lapse of more than fifteen years I cannot write the details of those awful and heartwringing days. Some things are too deep, too sacred for words.

In the May number of the *Burma News* appeared the following beautiful and just tribute, written by one who, of all men, knew Mr. Carson best:

ENTERED INTO REST

REVEREND ARTHUR E. CARSON,

Born, August 6, 1860. Died, April 1, 1908,
at Haka, Chin Hills, Burma

"BUT NOW ABIDETH FAITH, HOPE, LOVE, THESE THREE: BUT THE GREATEST OF THESE IS LOVE"

The saddest pleasure that ever comes to one is that of writing an obituary notice of his dearest friend a notice in which he seeks to give others little glimpses into those inner chambers where he himself has so long dwelt in delightful familiarity.

In all my life I have had only one very close friend. He is gone. And I realize that never again in this world shall I have another so close and dear as he has been for the last twenty-five years. We were chums in college and graduated together from the same class in theology. For two years in those old student days we kept house together, living in three little rooms, doing our own cooking and housework, eating and sleeping together. He had a prominent part in the services at my ordination and was officiating clergyman at my wedding. For over twenty years we have been missionaries together in Burma, the first six months living together in the same house and then for the next five years nearest missionary neighbors. During that first term we traveled and worked together a great deal on our over-lapping fields and very frequently went to each other's aid in hours of especial need. Our anniversaries of joy were celebrated together and we were with each other in help and sympathy in all hours of difficulty and sorrow. For many years we have kept up a regular correspondence with bi-weekly letters on each side. Probably no other two men in the Burma Mission have ever for so long a time known so much about each other's life and work.

Arthur E. Carson was born in Columbus City, Iowa, August 6, 1860. His parents were Americans of Irish descent and belonged to the well-to-do upper laboring class. He was taught the dignity and necessity of manual labor with actual experience therein from earliest childhood. He was ever proud of his ability to do things with his own hands and it is doubtful whether there has ever been a missionary in Burma more practically independent and self-helpful in those features of mission work that depend on manual labor.

His earlier education was in the American public schools—the most democratic institution on the face of the earth. He remained in school till fifteen years old, when he graduated from the High School in Morning Sun, Iowa.

In his sixteenth year the burden of the support of his father's family fell on him, his father having failed in both property and health at that time. Moving to the southwestern part of Nebraska, a homestead was taken, in the father's name and young Arthur supported the family by farming in summer and teaching country school through the winters.

At the age of twenty-two he entered the Gibbon (Nebraska) Seminary for college preparatory work and two years later went to Shurtleff College, Upper Alton, Illinois, for college and seminary work. Here he doubled up work, making good grades in all his classes, while, at the same time earning by outside work his entire support in school and the aid he regularly sent his parents. In June, 1886, he graduated from the Theological Department with the degree of B.D.

In the fall of 1886 he came to Burma, where he has wrought for God ever since with the exception of two furloughs (1896-7 and 1903-05) spent in America.

In December of this same year, 1886, he was married to Miss Laura Hardin, of the Sgaw Karen Mission, Bassein. They had been classmates in Gibbon Seminary and she, as affianced bride, had preceded him to Burma by three years. They have had two children, Carl Hardin Carson and Max Howard Carson—both now studying in Brown University, Providence, R. I.

Mr. and Mrs. Carson were the first regularly appointed missionaries to the Chins, tribes of Hill peoples in whom the Thomases had become interested in connection with Karen work at Henzada. For these tribes the Carsons have established and built up two pioneer stations in their twenty-two years of service.

It was more than a year after his arrival before a location was decided on and was ready for opening the new work. Meantime the Carsons, in the absence of other missionaries, looked after first the Henzada Karen work and afterwards the Prome Burman work. Thayetmyo was selected for the first station in the Chin Mission and here from 1888 till 1896 Mr. and Mrs. Carson slowly but steadily and solidly built up a magnificent work and got ready an adequate plant for its conduct. Their work was among the Chins of the lower hills and foothills of the Western Yomas, stretching through the Minbu, Thayetmyo and Henzada Districts on the west of the Irrawaddy with some villages in the Prome District on the east. In these eight years there were several hundreds of baptisms; the school grew from four Chin boarders to eighty-six Chin boarders, besides a number of Burman and other day pupils; and every Chin that had been in the school as long as six months had been converted. A number of young men had been given such training as was possible and were doing excellent work as evangelists while others were being given a better training in the Burman Seminary and in the Baptist College for more efficient service later on.

Almost from the beginning of his work in Thayetmyo, Mr. Carson became intensely interested in the then wild Chins in the higher and more northerly hills of the Western Yomas. It soon became an ambition that quickly grew into a determined purpose to plant a Mission in the Chin Hills, in the very midst of the untouched Chin masses of which those for whom he was working were but the Burmanized fringe.

This purpose was realized when, in March, 1899, Mr. and Mrs. Carson settled in Haka and began, first with interpreters but soon in native Chin, to proclaim the love of God and salvation through faith in Christ to a people who had no real idea of God, no adequate notion of sin, no worship whatever but individual, family or village offerings to evil spirits that they feared.

Soon Mrs. Carson was compelled to return to America and for over three years he stayed on absolutely alone, pushing the pioneer work, winning the confidence and good will of the Chins, only recently conquered and subdued by the white foreigners, acquiring a wonderful proficiency in their language, and building with his own hands, at an enormous saving to the Missionary Union's Treasury, an adequate mission plant—Mission dwelling house, school house, preacher's house, with all necessary outhouses.

In 1903, he turned the Haka Mission over to me (I held it for a year until Dr. East's return in 1904) and went to America for his second furlough. He had spent four years of the hardest work he had ever done in his life, most of the time in utter loneliness, without seeing any visible results or even any encouragement whatever among the people. It was not till his return from furlough nearly three years later, full seven years after the first occupation of Haka, that he baptized the first Haka convert and saw the school work begin to be appreciated by the Haka people.

Yet, through all those discouraging and lonely years, he never once lost heart or ever for a moment entertained a doubt as to success in his work here. And God honored his faith.

There had been four baptisms in other parts of the field previous to the first baptism at Haka, and the good results kept coming in with a steadily increasing ratio until he saw the one hundredth Chin convert here in the Chin Hills baptized just fifteen days before his death—sixty-four of the converts having been baptized within the last Associational year in answer to prayer for fifty baptisms. And everywhere in the field there is an interest in Christianity and a keen desire for education and other blessings introduced by the missionaries, that promises continued satisfactory success.

During the more than two years since his return from furlough, Mr. Carson, having no building operations on hand and relieved by his wife of all care and responsibility in the school work, has vigorously pushed evangelistic work. Undoubtedly his disease which had been in progress for a number of years was greatly aggravated and probably his death hastened by some recent difficult mountain travel in the prosecution of this evangelistic work. Meantime he had been diligently working out the beginnings of a literature in the dialect used by the Haka Chins. Part of this literary work he had submitted to Government for approval and since his death sanction has come from the Lieutenant-Governor for its introduction in the schools here, the alphabet being approved as he submitted it with a single suggested change.

An important feature of his life work that ought to be noticed is the work he did while at home on furlough. Few men have equaled him in loving to preach. It was one of the sacrifices of his life that he had so little opportunity to preach in his own native tongue. So both times when he went home on furlough he took pastorates of weak churches that satisfied his own two strongest desires—to do real mission work and to have the opportunity to regularly preach the gospel in English. At the same time he relieved the Missionary Union of the greater part of his home salary, though both he and his wife did a large amount of most valuable work for the Union among the churches and at associations, conventions and other denominational gatherings.

Mr. Carson was a many-sided man with many strong elements of character.

I think the most prominent feature of the man was virility. This it was that first and most powerfully struck strangers and ever remained prominent in his intercourse with friends. Sturdy, intrepid, forceful, he was one of the most manly men I have ever known: a born leader, always devotedly loved by his adherents and thoroughly respected by his opponents.

Scarcely less noticeable a feature of his character was positiveness. Doubts he may sometimes have had in the privacy of his own experiences; but never in the presence of others. Before he spoke he decided. He knew what he believed and why he believed it; and had absolute confidence in the processes by which he had arrived at his conclusions. It was undoubtedly the strongest element both in his preaching and in his ordinary conversation. After all, the world is never interested in doubts; never attracted by guesses, however brilliant; never moved by hesitant theories; but it is always impressed and swayed by positive convictions. No one ever heard my friend speak either in drawing-room or from the platform without feeling attracted and swayed by the positiveness of his convictions and the tense force of their expression.

He had, too, an active, capable intellect He did his own thinking. He read much and rather widely but no one ever recognized in his work matter taken from another—everything he gave out was stamped with his own individuality. He had had less training in language work than many other missionaries but few have equaled him in practical linguistic accomplishment in mission work. He not only mastered two widely different Chin languages so as to use them fluently and effectively in preaching and in difficult pioneer literary work but he used the Burmese, in which he never had to work directly, with more readiness and fluency than many Burman missionaries who have wrought for years in Burmese alone.

He was a man of strong faith. He believed God and relied absolutely, in every experience of life and service, on God's promises as found in the Bible. His was the old-fashioned faith that believed the Bible to be the very word of God without error of any kind except such minor and unimportant inaccuracies as still remain in man's work of handing down and translating the original manuscripts. He asked great things of God; he attempted great things for God: and he never wavered in his faith that his petitions would be granted, his work established. God honored his faith, too, though sometimes only after long and severe testing.

But to those of us who know him best the characteristic feature of his life was love. How strong, how abiding, that love was! It was a passion that almost scorched. Yet how gentle and tender! Virile, positive, combative as he was, his gentle sympathy and tender, clinging love were almost girlish—he had the heart and the touch of a young mother. No sacrifice was ever enough to try his love: no test of constancy could strain it. Never was a truer friend! Unable himself to admit a fault in one he loved, a criticism of his friend by another hurt him like a stab and at once put him on a stubborn defense. Love was, too, the most powerful force in his religious work. He got and held the hearts of his people. He literally loved into the Kingdom of God large numbers—many of whom were utterly unlovely in themselves.

But he had a way of finding something good and lovable in all and then hanging on to it and trusting it till he won out on it. All classes trusted him and believed in his friendship and he won the devotion of all—from the highest officials with whom he was brought in contact to the lowest, most uncouth savage among these Chins for whom he worked.

"But now abideth faith, hope, love, there three (and he had all in large measure); but the greatest of these is love."

H. H. Tilbe.

CHAPTER 22

CARRYING ON ALONE

How could I take up the work—*his* work—and carry it on without him? How many times he had put his hands on my shoulders and said, "My dear, we can do anything we have to. I can do all things through Christ, who strengtheneth me." I had worked with him on the translations, but he was a student and a scholar and I was neither, and I had depended upon him for every decision where scholarship was involved. We had worked out the alphabet of the language together and about a week after his home going the sanction of the Government for this alphabet was received.

New books must be made and printed. Dr. East's hands were more than full and this work fell to me. During the summer, Mrs. East developed trouble and it became apparent that she must go to America for operation. Accordingly in October they left for Rangoon, Dr. East intending when they left Haka to accompany his family to America.

Rev. and Mrs. J. H. Cope had been appointed to open up the work in Tiddim, near which place most of our Christians were located, and were on their way to Burma. Mrs. East stood the trip to Rangoon so well that it was decided after reaching there to send a nurse with her and her three little ones to America and for Dr. East to return to the Chin Hills with the Copes, who would not be able to do much with the work until they acquired some knowledge of the language. They came directly to Haka and lived with me while studying the language. During the months that I was alone, my hands were very full—mercifully so, for it gave little time to think of my loneliness. There was the school to superintend, some teaching to do, my sewing class, the

Sunday school lessons to translate, woman's meetings, daily interviews with visitors, quarrels to settle, and the medical work to look after, besides two hours of daily translation work on the gospels, and the housekeeping. These things so occupied my mind and heart during the day that I had little thought for anything else. But when night came it was different.

Because of their superstitions, believing that evil spirits are rampant at night, the Chins rarely go out after dark. Having no method of lighting their houses save by pine torches, they usually "go to bed with the chickens,"—and that is literal, for they keep their chickens in the house.

These custom's were a mercy to me, for they gave me evenings usually free from interruptions for reading and writing. I had no fear, but sometimes when the rain was heaviest such a sense of loneliness would overpower me that I could not read and I dare not write lest my letters should reveal this temporary mood which I wished to conceal from my friends.

On one such night as this when the rain was coming down in torrents, weary with the day's work, I sat listless and brooding, when about 9:30 there came a rap at my door and the Indian Telegraph operator came in with an urgent message. It was from Dr. East. On his way down country he had found a missionary with a very bad hand. He wanted certain medicine from a little medicine room in the top of the hospital and he wanted me not to fail in getting it off in the mail that left at daylight. This involved going to the cook house, getting the cook's smoky lantern (he had gone home), going through a veritable deluge of rain to the locked and dark hospital two blocks distant, climbing a very steep and long ladder to the top of the building, unlocking the medicine room and by the dim light of my dirty lantern searching for the medicine until I found it; returning to the house, searching through my storeroom for a suitable box in which to safely pack the medicine, going to the work shop for hammer and nails, packing, nailing up and addressing the box and then through the continued downpour climbing the very steep hill a quarter of a mile to the postoffice, arousing the Postmaster and making him promise to get the box off in the morning mail. I got home at eleven-thirty, my lonely mood gone—lost in service.

On another occasion just as I was preparing to retire late at night two huge torches glared in at my window from the dark night outside revealing two dusky faces peering in and the glitter of spears and guns. This startled me but proved to be nothing more serious than a letter sent in by the Superintendent and ordered to be delivered to me immediately upon arrival.

When the Assistant Superintendent was away on tour the people often came to me to settle their differences. On one such occasion two of the principal chiefs who had a long standing quarrel decided to come to me with it and promised each other to abide by my decision. I was able to settle the matter amicably so that both seemed satisfied. Upon hearing about it the Assistant Superintendent wrote me a very nice letter thanking me for being a "Peacemaker" among the people and at the same time saving him "a prodigious amount of work."

The leading Haka chief died and his youngest brother, according to Chin custom, succeeded to the chieftainship. He was only a boy and was in our school. We were trying hard to make him feel the responsibility of his position and try to make something of himself. A case came up in court in which he was interested. It went against him, he was impudent to the Assistant Superintendent and was promptly sent to jail. Knowing that if a case for insubordination came to trial against him it would be a serious matter, I rushed to the jail immediately upon hearing of it to see if there was anything I could do for the young man. The door was guarded by two huge Sikh soldiers with rifles. I told them I wanted to see Lien Tsum. They promptly opened the door and admitted me into his cell. He was lying on his face on the ground, frightened and weeping. I shall never forget the look on his face when he saw me in his cell. I showed him the seriousness of his offense and told him how wrong it was, even admitting the decision to have been unjust, to show disrespect to a higher official. He promised a humble apology and great care in the future.

I started to see the Assistant Superintendent to intercede for him before the case should be entered and this made impossible. When I left the jail the boy followed me out. The Sikh guard made no objections for was not this the Boinu! I could not ask them if it were permissible, for I knew no language that they did, so I took the chance and we marched through the town, I in front, the young chief next, and the two big Sikhs with their guns bringing up the rear. When the Assistant Superintendent saw us he came out, Lien Tsum made a most humble and appropriate apology, and to my great relief was forgiven and allowed to go home with the understanding that a second offense would have very grave results.

When the military officer who had charge of the jail learned that I had taken a prisoner out, he was greatly wrought up over the matter and said that if he had been there he would have had me arrested—but he wasn't there. To the day of his death, which occurred some two or three years later, Lien Tsum was my most loyal friend.

One day an old servant who had been in our employ for years came to me and said, "Boinu, I am in trouble. I don't know what to do." "What is it?" I said. "Can I help you?" "Well, a man has come from a distant village," he said, "and is demanding the price of my wife and I do not think it is just." "Why, Trum Harr," I answered in astonishment, "can it be that you have been working in the mission all these years and have not yet paid for your wife?"

He looked very sheepish as he dropped his eyes and said, "Why, don't you know, Boinu, how I got my wife?" "No," I said, "I have never heard anything about it." "Well, it was like this," he explained, still looking at his feet. "My wife was an orphan and lived at her uncle's and while she was only a young girl, people said she had the evil eye and bewitched folks. So they drove her out of the village to die. She wandered about the jungle and finally came to Haka. After being here for a short time, some people came from her village and saw her. 'Don't you know that girl has the evil eye and bewitches people? She can keep your crops from growing, your stock from reproducing and cause death and destruction among your people. We drove her from our village,' they said. When the chiefs heard this they called a council and decided the girl must die. She slipped away secretly and came to me and begged me to save her. I was a poor man and had no money to buy a wife; besides, I felt very sorry for her, so I hid her away and she became my wife.

"Then I got work at the mission and had some money and after a long time my wife began to go out among people and nobody said anything, and finally the chiefs had another council and decided she no longer had the evil eye (they wanted to borrow my money) and since then we have been very happy and you know we have three children. But her uncle heard that she was still living, that the chiefs said she no longer had the evil eye, and that I had money so he has come and demands that I pay the price of a girl of her station. He drove her out to die. I saved her life, and have supported her ever since. I don't think I ought to have to pay for her," he said with a very troubled face. I did not think so either, and they finally settled it by his giving her people a feast.

CHAPTER 23

A LEPER'S FATE AND THE SEQUEL

One morning a sturdy little woman appeared at the Mission Hospital bearing on her back her leper husband. She had carried him over the mountains in this way for more than fifty miles! She would stagger along for a little way, then rest and go on again, camping out nights wherever dark overtook her.

Dr. East received her with great kindness, but told her that her husband must be segregated or he would endanger others; that he could be helped but not cured. The doctor had a cozy little grass hut built for the poor man, furnished him with nourishing food and did everything possible for his comfort. The poor wife trudged back over the mountains to her home.

For a time the man seemed happy and cheerful, for he had more comforts than ever before in his life and he rapidly improved in health. But after a time, not being allowed to mingle with others, he became very lonely and begged to be allowed to return home.

Dr. East made a trip to a neighboring village and during his absence the leper heard that a man and boy were going to his village. He secretly left and started with them. We missed him but could get no clew to his whereabouts until the mail coolies coming in from Falam the next morning reported that they had seen a dead man by the roadside some ten or twelve miles from Haka. We at once surmised it was the leper Christian, and Mr. Cope started at once to ride out and see. A few hours later a note came in from him saying that it was indeed the leper, that it would be late before he would be able to get the body carried in and for me to make such preparations as I could for the funeral.

In the loft of the school house there were some good pine boards which my husband had had sawed and put away for just such an emergency. I had some taken down and carried to the workshop, then told the boys who had helped me that the leper Christian was dead and for them to call the only Chin man who knew how to handle a saw, to come and help make a coffin for him; also to send two other men who did odd jobs for the mission, to dig a grave.

I waited and called but no one came. I went to the school house and found that all of the older pupils had mysteriously disappeared. I went back to the workshop and began to measure and cut boards myself. While thus engaged the only Burmese man in Haka, a Buddhist of more or less education, who had a position under Government, came along and seeing me at work with my saw, stopped to inquire what I was doing. I told him of the death of the leper who was soon to be brought in for burial, and of my inability to find any one to help me.

He said, "There are many beliefs about lepers. That is why the people will not come to help you. If I were among my own people, I could not help you either, but I cannot see you, a white lady, do this hard work alone. I know it is not your custom. I will help you." And he did. While we were working on the coffin, I talked of our religious beliefs and he seemed very much interested. I asked him if I would give him some literature in his own language telling him more about it if he would read it. He said he would be delighted to do so. I selected some of the best tracts we had and gave him several.

About dusk the body of the leper was brought in, being carried on a stretcher by coolies. Dr. East returned about the same time. Not a Chin was in evidence anywhere: Dr. East and Mr. Cope, Aung Dwe (our Christian Karen teacher who said the Chins were all afraid to come near) and Shwe Bwin, the Burman had to go and dig the grave, which, in the very hard, stony soil, was no small job.

By the light of lanterns they carried the poor leperous remains of a freed soul to the grave and buried it.

The next morning the man for whom I had sent to help me make the coffin came and I asked him why he had refused to come when I sent for him the day before. "Boinu, [an honorific title given to the wives of big chiefs] I have worked for you for thirteen years, haven't I? And

I have never refused to do a thing you asked me before, have I? Boinu, you do not understand how we feel about lepers. We cannot go near a leper corpse nor have a thing to do with burying one. If we did, our feet would swell and burst, and we would leave tracks of blood wherever we went. Why, those men who carried that man in yesterday would have died rather than carry him if they had known he was a leper."

"But, Sun Hkwa," I said, "there is a leper down in the village. What will you do when he dies? Leave him to lie and rot where he dies?" "No, our custom is like this," he said. "When he dies his wife will have to go to the forks of a stream and dig a grave and then come back and get her dead husband, carry him on her back to the grave, put him in, then take off all her clothes and bury them with him. Some of her friends will meet her on the way home with a blanket. The priest will go to her house and sacrifice a hog in it and then she can go back there to live, but nobody must go near the house until the sacrifice has been made." "Well," I said, "suppose the wife dies before he does, then what would you do?" "In that case," he said, "the whole village would contribute to hire an idiot or half-witted person to carry the body to the forks of a stream and bury it. I am sorry I could not do what you asked, Boinu. There is nothing else I would refuse to do; but I would die rather than help bury a leper." And yet they mingle with them in closest relations while living, absolutely without fear.

A few days after the leper's funeral Shwe Bwin, the Burman, came saying that he had read the tracts with great interest and would like some more. I had a nice talk with him, gave him more tracts, got a Burmese New Testament, marked passages in it, gave that to him also and asked him to come to our Sunday services. This he promised to do, though I had little hope of his coming, for the Burmans consider themselves far superior to the other races of the country.

When Sunday came, however, Shwe Bwin was there and he came regularly afterwards and finally asked for baptism. His wife, he said, refused to cook a morsel of food for him on Sundays, and felt deeply humiliated and disgraced because of his association with "the dirty Chins."

Shwe Bwin read his Bible with great interest and often came to talk to our Karen teacher and to me of what he read. Dr. East and

Mr. Cope knew no Burmese and he knew no English, so they were unable to help him. Nevertheless I have rarely seen any one more interested in anything than that man became in his Bible. His youngest son became very ill and he sent for me. I saw that the child was very sick and remained for the night, doing what I could for his comfort. But the time came when we all thought he was dying. The mother held him on her knees. With a look of agony, she said, "I have sacrificed and sacrificed, and it did no good. Pray, oh, pray to your God and if he lets my child live, I will worship him till I die!" Shwe Bwin and I both knelt and prayed asking God, if it could be his will, to show his power over death and strengthen the mother's awakening faith. When we arose from our knees the child had dropped into a natural sleep and from that time on continued to improve until strong and well.

Was that answer to prayer? Or did the crisis just happen to come at that hour? Anyhow, the woman believed it was answer to prayer. She never afterwards refused to cook her husband's food but came with him to church, and a few months later was baptized. Shwe Bwin himself gave up his Government job and went back to the plains to preach the Gospel among his own people. The missionary who employed him told me that he became one of the most effective evangelists that ever worked on his field.

CHAPTER 24

NEW RECRUITS AND THIRD RETURN

Shortly after the arrival of the Copes, an English lady tourist who prided herself in finding her way into the most remote and out-of-the-way places in the world, put in an appearance at our mission. It was a great event to see somebody from the outside world. But on the very day of her arrival, a man wearing a great, black plume in his hair, carrying a gun and looking wild-eyed and frightened appeared at my door. The plume was evidence that he had killed somebody; for no one except a human slayer was permitted to wear the great, black plumes prized beyond any other earthly possession—except a gun. The man asked to speak to me privately. I took him into my study and shut the door. His first words were, "I have killed my wife. You have influence with the English Government. I want you to save my life. You can if you will. You are just like a god." "But how did this happen?" I asked. "Well, I got drunk and we quarreled and I threw a stick of wood at her and killed her. I did not intend to hit her. I meant only to frighten her; but it struck her and killed her and now I want you to save me. I will do anything you tell me to do," he said. I talked to him trying to make him realize what an awful thing he had done and advised him to turn himself over to the authorities and to tell them the exact truth in the matter. He said he would do whatever I advised, so I wrote a note to the British Officer who soon came down with a guard and took him in charge. The lady tourist was not sure but that she had got farther from the "beaten tracks" than she had counted on—especially as some men came in shortly after carrying the stuffed skin of a huge panther which they had recently killed.

During the rains that season (1909) Dr. East had serious heart trouble and became convinced that he could not remain long at that high altitude. Mr. Cope was preparing to make his headquarters at Tiddim in the northern part of our field, where by far the largest number of our Christians were located.

Day after day Dr. East was obliged to keep to his bed while teaching his preachers' training class. Finally Dr. and Mrs. Woodin were appointed to take up the medical work and Dr. East was relieved to go home. The Copes went to Tiddim. With these four young people fresh from America and full of enthusiasm for the work, we hoped for great results. Mrs. Cope worked with the children and interested herself in young mothers with babies, giving them many a useful lesson, and in her quiet way ministering to their needs and incidentally winning her way into every heart. Mrs. Woodin with her sweet voice, musical talent and aptness in acquiring the language soon had a large place in the affections of the people. Both men worked hard and conscientiously and great good was accomplished. Progress in the work at Tiddim was especially gratifying as the people, a different tribe, were more intelligent, less drunken, and were eager for education and progress. The Woodins were greatly handicapped in that Mrs. Woodin never had a well day after reaching Haka. I stood with the doctor beside her bed when it seemed only a miracle could save her. God gave her back to us, in answer to prayer, and she worked bravely on, though never well.

In the spring of 1912, I returned to America on furlough in company with Mrs. E. B. Roach and her little five-year-old daughter, Evelyn. Ralph Henderson, then a lad in knee breeches, was entrusted to my care for the home trip, being sent to be with his sister in that wonderful home in Newton Center, presided over by "Mother West." His intelligent interest in the wonderful sights we saw added much to the pleasure of the trip for me. But I remember his coming to me one day with a very crestfallen look on his face and asking me if I thought I could mend his best trousers, saying that he had been scuffling with a boy and had split them "from Maine to Texas," and so he had.

We went from Rangoon to Colombo where we spent a week on the matchless island of Ceylon, then took ship for Naples and from Naples went directly across to New York. When we reached Naples the children were so delighted to get on shore that as soon as possible we took them out for a walk. At the entrance of the Public Garden not far from our hotel there was a statue of Victor Emmanuel. When little Evelyn saw it she exclaimed, "Oh, Mamma, see that big idol with truly trousers on!" All the many idols she had seen before were of Gautama Boodha, and therefore not of the kind that wore trousers. While waiting for our steamer we went to Pompeii and spent an entrancing day among its buried wonders. We also went to the top of Vesuvius and peered into her smoking crater.

One never-to-be-forgotten week we spent in Rome, filling each day to overflowing with sight-seeing. While drinking in the beauty of a marvelous collection of statuary in the Vatican little Evelyn broke the spell of our rapture by saying, "Let's go home. I'm sick of all these old idols."

We drove out on the Appian Way to the Three Taverns and imagined we could see Paul meeting with the brethren. We went into the catacombs and tried to realize what the early Christians endured for a faith more precious than life. We stopped for a day at Palermo on the island of Sicily and drove through lemon groves several miles out into the country to a famous old cathedral. Here also we visited the catacombs where, up to within twenty years before, they had placed their dead. Bodies were put in a large tank of chemicals and kept for two months, then taken out and, dressed as in life, were placed in little niches, with glass doors, along the passageways. The vision of a bride in all her wedding finery haunts me yet as I recall that day! It seemed to me a peculiar people that could make an exhibition of the sacred bodies of their dead. It seemed sacrilege to be there, and we hurried away. We saw many quaint and thrilling objects during that eventful day.

Upon my arrival in New York, I was met by both of my sons, now men doing for themselves. After graduating at Brown University, Carl went to Paris for a year for the study of International Law at the Sarbonne, and was now teaching in Port Washington, New York. Max, though not yet through with his technical education, was working with the engineers on the great Lackawanna Bridge at Nicholson, Pennsylvania. What a visit I had with them! I left them as lads. I found them taking their places as men in the work of the world.

During the summer I went to Nebraska and Idaho to visit relatives; then to Southern California to spend the greater part of my furlough with my brothers and sisters and my dear old mother, then past ninety years of age. Carl applied for and secured a position in Pasadena. He was married to Miss Gertrude O'Neill of Yonkers, New York, the following summer and came to California to live. We persuaded Max to come to Throop College of Technology, Pasadena, for his technical work, so we might all be together during the remainder of my furlough. Though both mother and sister were very critically ill during this time, I had the satisfaction of being permitted to nurse them and both were restored to reasonable health; so it seemed that my furlough was opportune and we were all so happy to be together. It was rather a unique experience, making the acquaintance of my own sons, but it proved to be a very delightful one.

During the terrible scourge of influenza following the great war Carl's wife, Gertrude, became a victim of that dread disease and died in New York City after a brief illness. Carl afterwards married Miss Mary Agnes Dempsey, of Philadelphia, who is the proud mother of his two beautiful children.

Max graduated from the course in Civil Engineering at Throop School of Technology, Pasadena, California, in 1916, and was that same year married to Miss Lillian Jane Sutherland, youngest daughter of Dr. George Sutherland, for many years President of Grand Island College (Nebraska). Later he entered the Federal service and was sent to Honolulu, which I found rather a good place to visit on my final return to America.

CHAPTER 25

BACK TO THE FIELD AGAIN

In the autumn of 1914, in company with Rev. and Mrs. Davenport of Maulmain, I turned my face once more towards the Chin Hills. Just before leaving, my church people (the First Church, Pasadena) gave me a reception and shower. Besides many useful and beautiful gifts one of the members at parting put into my hand fifty dollars "for personal comforts on the voyage" and a dear member of the Calvary Church sent me another fifty dollars "for the work." Little did the givers think at the time that their gifts would save from intense suffering from hunger the lives of so many of our Christians. But this will appear later.

We sailed by the Pacific route calling at Yokohama, Kobe, Nagasaki, Shanghai, Manila, Hongkong, Saigon, and Singapore. Being in the early days of the war this route was considered safer than crossing the Atlantic. In mid-ocean we heard by wireless of the destruction of the German cruiser *Emden* which had last been heard of in Pacific waters and which already had to her credit the sinking of seventy-five thousand tons of British shipping. For three nights we had run without lights and it was a great relief to know that we had nothing further to fear from her.

Upon our arrival in Yokohama, we were invited by the Japanese President of the Steamship Company to tea in his magnificent palace in Tokyo the following afternoon. We eagerly accepted and were furnished with dainty badges which were to be worn on that occasion. Arriving at the station, we were met by private jinrikisha men who recognized the guests by the badges and soon had us seated in luxurious jinrikishas and on the way to the palace.

At the door we were met by servants who had us sit while they drew cloth stockings over our shoes—for no unprotected shoes must enter that wonderful palace which is built of the most exquisite polished wood and without a nail in the entire building. The owner of the palace knew no English, but he and his wife received us with many bows and smiles. A young Japanese woman who had spent several years in New York was summoned and took us in charge. First we were taken upstairs and served tea in Japanese fashion, being instructed by the young lady that the handleless cups were to be held with both hands and that only three sips were to be taken at a time. This rather painful performance over, we were given souvenirs of dainty-colored candies which, it was explained, wished us friendship, prosperity and long life.

We were then taken to an upper veranda from which we had a charming view, then through the palace into a museum where there was a remarkable collection of all things Japanese, many of them said to be thousands of years old and many of entrancing beauty. There were tapestries, carvings, inlaid work, paintings, exquisite china, rare old vases of cloisonne and satsuma centuries old and thousands of other things that beggar description.

We were finally taken to a very large drawing room richly furnished in English style, and here on inlaid tables with priceless china we were served a sumptuous English "high tea" while we listened to a Japanese prima donna and enjoyed the very clever feats of a Japanese past master in legerdemain. As we passed out of the door, our host, smiling and bowing, presented us with souvenirs of our visit in the form of photographs of the palace. It was a wonderful day—like a dream of fairyland.

We dined with the Dearings and had tea with Miss Converse in Yokohama, lunched with the Thompsons in Kobe, spent Sunday and visited the Methodist mission in Nagasaki, and upon our arrival in Manila we docked alongside of the German cruiser *Geier*, which we afterwards learned was out after the very steamer we were on when her boilers became disabled and she was forced to put into Manila for repairs.

Two days later we received a wireless message that the *Geier* had been interned by the United States Government as the Japanese had learned that she was there and had two warships watching the port so she was unable to get away by the allotted time. Our (Japanese) steamer was delayed by provisioning the warships which watched the harbor.

From Manila we went to Hongkong, in the same steamer in which we sailed from San Francisco and which was convoyed across the Pacific by two Japanese warships. We had, as fellow passengers, the retiring Governor of the Philippines and his wife.

Hongkong was under martial law at that time and we had to go to the Provost Marshal, produce our passports and get his permission before we could leave the city. We took passage on a French steamer for Singapore and stopped for a day and a half at Saigon (Cochin China), where the American Consul called upon us and invited us to the Consulate to tea, and did much to make our short visit a pleasure. I had the pleasure of meeting the same man a few years later, then our Consul in Rangoon, Burma—Mr. Laurence Briggs.

It was at Saigon that we first began to fully realize the awful grief and suffering caused by the war. Here we took on French soldiers and officers going to the front. The scene was a deeply pathetic one. There were women in deepest mourning, to see them off, wringing their hands and weeping; and brave French officers kissed one another and shed tears at parting. Well they knew that few were likely to return.

In Singapore, because of the war, they would give us no shipping information whatever, but advised us to go to Penang by rail from which place it might be possible to get to Rangoon by local coast steamer. The trip across from Singapore to Penang took us through extensive tin mines and large rubber plantations. Some of the scenery was very beautiful and the whole of the trip was full of interest. In Penang we put up at a hotel in plain view of the spars of the Russian cruiser and French destroyer sunk only a short time before by the German cruiser *Emden*, which, disguised by an extra smokestack and flying the Japanese flag boldly steamed into the harbor past British guns one morning and torpedoed both of these vessels and got away before anybody knew what was happening.

We were detained a whole week in Penang, and were unable to get one word of shipping information. Mr. Davenport cabled Mr. Phinney, our mission treasurer, as to what route to take if any were obtainable.

Regular steamers were running between Calcutta and Rangoon. He therefore replied, "Take Calcutta then Rangoon." Less than a half hour after this cable message was received we were all three called before the chief of police that he might inquire into the matter as to who were going to "take Calcutta and Rangoon!" Eventually a shipping agent came and told us to come at once and he would get us aboard a small coast steamer which would sail almost immediately. We had to pay a third more than the usual fare and although the little craft was greatly overcrowded and uncomfortable (men slept both on and under the dining-room table) we were thankful enough to get away—without "taking" Calcutta!

We reached Rangoon December 18th, 1914, and were warmly welcomed by the missionaries. We learned that we must leave our photographs with the American Consul, have a similar one put upon our passports, and then get special passports for traveling in Burma from the Commissioner of Police before we would be allowed to leave Rangoon. Several busy days were spent in Rangoon buying and packing stores, but finally, on January 6th, I got off for the Chin Hills, thankful enough to be on the last lap of the journey begun ten long weeks before.

As I crossed on the ferry at Amarapoora Shore for Sagaing, I counted without changing my seat seventy-nine pagoda spires in sight at the same time.

Mr. and Mrs. Grigg met me in Sagaing and we crossed the river to Ava and viewed the spot where the noble "Ann of Ava" and her martyr husband, Dr. Judson, had suffered beyond measure for the cause they loved. A memorial tablet to the Christian hero and martyr had recently been placed there.

Mr. Cope met me at Kalewa. As he had only one pony, we had to "ride and tie" on the trip up the mountains, though he would gladly have walked all the way if I had allowed it. The first stage was sixteen miles, seven of which I walked. The shortest stage on the whole trip to Tiddim was eight miles. The longest one—a double stage—was twenty-nine miles. I got pretty tired when the road was very steep, but on the whole enjoyed it. The entire journey was full of interest.

At Kalemyo we were told that a tiger had a few days before killed two bullocks of a pack train and so frightened the others that two more were rushed over a cliff and killed. At the next station, called No. 3, we were told that a man had recently been killed by a tiger and a few days later two men, one of whom was carrying a bag of millet, were attacked. While one man freed himself from the bag of millet, the other man beat the tiger over the head with a club. The tiger absconded with the bag of millet and both men got away! At the next station we were told of a man who shot a bear and wounded it. The bear started for him; he dropped on the ground, covered his head with his blanket, and lay as if dead. The bear clawed him dreadfully, tearing out one of his eyes, but finally left him.

All the way up the mountains, we were frequently greeted by little bands of Siyin Christians. How good it seemed to be among them again!

The Woodins met us at Fort White and we all went on together to attend the Association at Tiddim. After excellent meetings and the joyful greeting of many Christians, the Woodins and I wended our way on to Haka. Because of Mrs. Woodin's sensitiveness to the sun, we were obliged to get up at two or three o'clock mornings and make our marches before the sun was high. In the freshness of the morning, these early rides through wooded hills were delightful. On one occasion our ponies stopped stock-still and refused to be urged forward. They trembled with fear. Mrs. Woodin riding in front called back to her husband. At the sound of her voice a huge animal leaped across our path into the dense jungle. We got only a shadowy view of it in the pale moonlight, but we had vivid mental pictures of the man-eating tiger of which we had heard in that vicinity only a few days before. Two miles out from Haka, we were met by the entire school and many of the Christians, who gave me a welcome that warmed my heart.

CHAPTER 26

MEETING NEW PROBLEMS

With my return the Woodins, in correspondence with the Reference Committee because of Mrs. Woodin's continued ill health and being loath to give up the work and return to America, decided to try another station; and as soon as they could pack up after my arrival they transferred to Bhamo. Mr. Cope came back, with his family, to Haka for headquarters while he took charge of the entire Chin Hills field. Mrs. Cope took charge of the Hospital and housekeeping and superintended the schools in the Tiddim district while I managed the schools in the Haka district, looked after the work among the women and gave as much time as possible to the translation of the gospels and again took up the weekly translation of the Sunday School lessons.

My house was sadly out of repair on my return. The roof was off and the beaver board ceiling and partitions had been taken down for preservation. I think Dr. Woodin got the corrugated iron roof on before he left. I know that I got a Chin man to help me tack on the beaver board, then to prevent the swelling and shrinking and so cracking the beautiful new wall paper I had brought from America I pasted strips of cheese cloth around every one of the yard square boards in the five rooms of that house—including ceilings. Then I cut and put on every strip of paper. It was a hard job for a woman of elephantine proportions, but when it was all done and the pretty new curtains, given me by the ladies of the First Church of Santa Ana, California, were up, I had a home of which I was prouder than any queen in her royal palace.

But before many months the little son of the Copes' was taken ill. He did not seem to recover as he should, their furlough was due and they decided, if any arrangement could be made for the work, to go home on short leave. Miss Agnes Whitehead, a capable and successful self-supporting missionary of Maulmain, feeling the urgency of the need, generously offered to come and stay with me during their absence. We gladly accepted her offer and Mr. Cope went down the mountains to meet her. While he was gone little Harry grew worse. The day they were expected to arrive his condition grew so serious that we sent a messenger out to meet them, urging Mr. Cope to make all possible haste. We had telegraphed to Falam—thirty-five miles over steep mountain roads, for the only doctor in the Chin Hills. He had arrived that morning and said that pneumonia had set in and that the end was near. He had come too late! Mr. Cope left Miss Whitehead to come on with the natives and he hastened home with all speed, getting there only an hour or so before the precious little life went out. A pine coffin was made by a Chinaman and Miss Whitehead and I padded, lined and covered it. Mr. Cope himself conducted the brief and tender service in the language of our people, and we laid our darling to rest under the shadow of the pines. Five days later Mr. and Mrs. Cope and their remaining son started on the long voyage to America. Miss Whitehead and I were alone until the return of Mr. Cope, without his wife, ten months later.

One incident that occurred during this time is worthy of mention. Our Postmaster was a Hindu with a fairly good knowledge of English. One evening I received a note from him saying that he was "very much confused in regard to religious matters" and asked me to lend him the best book I had on Christianity. I sent him a New Testament with marked passages and chapters and asked him to come down and have a talk with us, stating a time when we could see him. His note closed with this sentence: "If I can get help I will very much thank you and God."

He came at the appointed time and we (Miss Whitehead and I) had a long talk with him. He said he was tired of a "man-made religion with its millions of gods and senseless caste system" and seemed open to the truth. We asked if we might pray for him and he said "Yes," so we all three knelt and both Miss Whitehead and I prayed that he might find the truth with its accompanying peace of mind and heart. The next morning early he came back saying he had been reading the little book I gave him (the New Testament) and found where a rich young man had come to Christ and asked what he must do to be saved; and that Christ had said, "Sell all you have and give to the poor and come and follow Me." "I am not rich," he said, "but I do not want to be like that young man. I have brought a hundred rupees which I want to give Mamma for Christian work." I explained to him that he must not think he could buy salvation, but he seemed to understand that. When I took the money and thanked him for it, "No, no!" he said. "Do not thank me—thank God."

A few days later he came with a beaming face. He said that he believed Christ was the son of God and that the Christian religion was true! But a shadow came over his face when he said that being baptized into the Christian church would mean giving up all his people—all that was dear to him in the world—and that he could never enter his own village again.

Before he left we prayed with him again, after which he stepped to the door and produced a huge bundle which proved to be twenty new blankets which he wanted to donate to our Boys' Dormitory, saying again that he did not want to be like "the rich young man." Only two or three days later I got a note from him saying he had been transferred with the Expeditionary Force to Mesopotamia. I wrote to him there and the following is a quotation from his reply. "Rest assured I want to hear from you more earnestly about the work and teaching of Christ the most holy and true God and Saviour of mankind. True Mamma to say how gracious and kind our Lord. Happy are they who are blessed to kiss the dust of his feet—the true God of love, light and perfect salvation. Yours fondly—"

I never saw him again, but believe he had found the "peace that passeth understanding."

As Mrs. Cope did not return with her husband Miss Whitehead consented to stay another year. She was greatly handicapped by not knowing the language of our people and felt that she was accomplishing but little, yet I do not know how we would have survived that year without her cheery presence and help.

CHAPTER 27

NATIVE INSURRECTION—
DURING WORLD WAR

As a baby boy had been born to Mrs. Cope she decided to remain in America another year before undertaking the long voyage alone with her baby. Miss Whitehead, feeling that she could not remain a third year, returned to her work in Maulmain. Before Mr. Cope returned from taking her down the mountains word came that the Government was going to attempt to raise "a coolie corps" from among our people, for service in France. This caused great excitement. One corps had already been raised among the Siyins in Tiddim and efforts were being made to raise another in the Falam subdivision. Haka would be next! All military British officers and sepoys who could be spared had been withdrawn from the Hills and had gone to France. Civil officers were sent to lower Burma for military training. Haka was therefore left without a British officer and with only a handful of sepoys, most of whom were mere boys, no one dreaming that the Haka Chins would make any serious trouble. But there was an undercurrent of tense excitement. One could feel it in the air. There were only three English-speaking people in Haka at the time, two Anglo-Indian men and myself. There was a rumor of trouble and attempted revolt in Falam and our Haka civil officer was hastily recalled from lower Burma, and the sepoy guard for Haka was increased from twenty-six to fifty men.

Upon his return the Assistant Superintendent called upon me, told me of the trouble they were having in Falam, but said that he did not anticipate any trouble in Haka. He called in his chiefs from the various villages, told them of the need of their services to Britain and of the generous terms offered, and then told each chief, according to the number of villages, he "ate" (or governed), the number of men he must furnish. The Government orders were that no coercion was to be used; but the chiefs did not understand that. An order to bring in the men meant that *they must bring them*. Chief after chief came to me and asked what he should do. They said that their people absolutely refused to go to France; that they said they had no quarrel with Germany and why should they go and fight the Germans? They said they would commit suicide rather than go.

One evening Shia Kaw, our first Haka Christian convert, who was teaching school in the large village of Sakta, twenty miles distant, appeared at the Mission closely followed by two Sakta Chins. He made me understand that he wanted to speak to me in private. The men were watching his every move. After casually talking to him for a few moments I stepped into my storeroom and called to him to come and get some rice I had for him. Understanding the ruse he came quickly saying as he took the rice, "I will come to-night. I have something to tell you" and hastened back, meeting the two Sakta men following into the store-room. It was very evident they did not intend he should have any private conversation with me. After the Chins had gone to bed Shia Kaw slipped softly in at my back door, saw that the blinds were closely drawn and then shaking with excitement said that if the Sakta Chins knew what he was going to tell me they would certainly kill him. He said that thirteen villages had united, taking the sacred oath that they would attack Haka, kill the sepoys, take their guns and with them clear the Hills of the British and resume their own government. He said that the men of Sakta had secreted their women and children in the jungle and carried out six months' provision for them, and that they were spending their time day and night making ammunition; that two days before six hundred armed men had congregated less than three miles from Haka with plans all made for an attack; but that he and Maung Lun, a Karen preacher in the employ of the Mission, had told them of the strength of the British and of their own certain ultimate defeat and had persuaded them to disband and return to their villages. But upon their return they were so derided by their friends over the outcome of the wonderful things they had boasted they would do that they were planning to gather in larger members and to be met in the North by an equally large force. "And if they do, God pity us, for we will every one be killed," he said, tragically striking his breast with both hands. Maung Lun was not permitted to come to Haka lest he give information. About this time an exodus of our school boys began—all the boys from a certain village would suddenly disappear from school during the night. The next night another group would disappear. This had never occurred before and I knew that only a matter of serious nature would induce them to leave without my knowledge or permission. Our school dwindled to a mere handful and there was suppressed excitement everywhere. The Assistant Superintendent sent out orders for the school children to return but without response.

Mr. Cope, to my great relief, returned from Rangoon. I told him all I knew of conditions and he went up to have a conference with the Assistant Superintendent. He felt that my fears were ungrounded; said that he had made investigation and found that the things Shia Kaw told were untrue; that the Sakta people were loyal to the Government and that he had received a list of ninety names of Sakta men who were keen to go to France. The next afternoon Shia Kaw came in again saying that forces were collecting again, both north and south of us, and that Haka was to be attacked within the next three or four days. I told him that the Assistant Superintendent said he had investigated and found conditions in Sakta normal; that women and children had not been taken away; that the people were loyal and that at least ninety were ready to go to France, and that there would be no insurrection. He was greatly excited and distressed and begged us to heed the warning which he had risked his life to bring. That night the Christians asked permission to sleep in the Mission Hospital and Mr. Cope and the teachers patrolled the Mission property all night—but there was no disturbance.

The following evening they were afraid even to sleep in the Hospital, fearing it would be burned, and asked to sleep in the cellars of the two Mission houses. Here and in my study they huddled frightened and shivering. In the early evening Tsan Dwe, a Christian young man who belonged to an important chief's family, came and told us that there was no doubt but that an attack would be made, for his brother had seen a large force congregated that evening only about three miles from Haka. Mr. Cope immediately informed the Assistant Superintendent but he was still incredulous. He said that Shia Kaw was an alarmist and had got the people so stirred up that they were imagining all sorts of things. However, he would investigate. Mr. Cope came home and again patrolled the Mission property. Just at dawn he received a note from the Assistant Superintendent saying he had made investigation and had learned that all Shia Kaw had told us was true; that the Saktas had deceived him and that forces were gathered both north and south of us and that doubtless an attack would soon be made. Mr. Cope came and told me and we sat down to an early breakfast while talking things over. During the night, amid the mob of men, women and children in his cellar, a little child was born to the wife of one of our teachers. He is called Ral Zam (Fleeing from the Enemy).

Before we had half finished breakfast there came a messenger from the Assistant Superintendent saying that we must hasten into the Police Lines; that an army of 5,000 were advancing and would reach Haka within an hour or two. Mr. Cope immediately hastened from the table to look after the Christians. He had barely gone when a second messenger came saying that it was the order of the Assistant Superintendent that "The Boinu" (I am the Boinu) "hasten into the Police Lines." What was I to do? The poor woman with the two hours' old baby could not be left. Her husband had gone to their home on some errand, and there seemed to be no help available. All was confusion and excitement. A third messenger came with peremptory orders. "The Boinu *must* go to the Police lines immediately!" My cook came around at last, a big, strong man. He put his hands on his knees and, well wrapped in a blanket, we got the new mother on his back and started up the hill. I called a passing school boy, wrapped little Ral Zam in another blanket, gave him to the boy and sent him to follow the mother. Then I went to my store room and collected such food as we could carry. Mr. Cope, having done all that he could for the Christians, came and we slowly climbed the steep hill, hearing several shots fired as we went. The "Police Lines" meant a few government buildings with a trench around them. In this trench were placed our sepoys with their guns. They were so few in number that our Karen teachers and a few Christian Chins who had guns joined them. The best building in the Lines was the station Hospital—a brick building with a small office room, a tiny medicine room and two fair-sized wards. One of these wards was taken for the white population of Haka, consisting of the Assistant Superintendent, Mr. Cope, Major Newland (a retired army officer), his grown son, and myself. The other was reserved for the sick and wounded. In that room we lived, ate, and slept, for twenty-two days and nights. The first two or three nights there were twenty-two of us who slept in that one room. But after that the Assistant Superintendent succeeded in getting the native Christians who were with us into other quarters. There was no means of privacy and for six nights I did not even have my shoes off; but after that the Assistant Superintendent very kindly had the little closet-like medicine room cleared for me and a cot put in it. I think I have never been more grateful for anything in my life. The place was so small that I could barely crowd in, in front of the cot, and there was an opening in the wall into the fireplace in the ward where cooking was constantly going on, so that the room was dense with smoke which nearly blinded me; yet no woman was ever more thankful for a marble palace than was I for that little room which gave me a bit of privacy.

No attack was made that first day. The next morning fifteen mounted sepoys were sent out to reconnoiter, followed by the Assistant Superintendent and a few foot soldiers. They were fired upon by ambushed men to the number of about fifty. The Chins, having only muzzle-loading guns, after firing, immediately disappeared into the dense jungle where the mounted men could not follow. The Assistant Superintendent was recalled by a messenger madly riding up to say that a force of 5,000 men was advancing from the opposite direction. He hastily returned to protect the station, but no further advance was made during the day. In the early evening there was furious firing for a few moments from the surrounding jungles which was returned by the men in the trenches, then all was quiet for the remainder of the night.

The next morning we were told to go, under a strong guard, back to the Mission and gather up a few valuables, some clothing and such food as we could get and a quantity of firewood, and have our school boys carry the things within the Lines. While getting the things together we heard two gun shots quite near and Chins ran wildly into our compound, waving green branches above their heads which was evidently a signal of loyalty to the attacking force. Presently there was a sharp firing from the Lines and we hastened up the hill. We were met at the top by the Assistant Superintendent, who said, "For God's sake hurry, Mrs. Carson. The sergeant's wife has been shot and killed and his daughter has also been shot and is in a dying condition. She is calling for you with every breath." I hurried to her. She was a fine Christian girl of seventeen who had been staying with me nights. "Oh, my dear Boinu," she said, "I shall never go to school any more, but God will receive my spirit." She then begged her Buddhist father to become a Christian and meet her in Heaven, and asked me to pray for her. I held her head in my arms until God released her spirit.

The next day we arranged to give her a Christian burial, but scarcely had we got outside the Lines on the way to the cemetery before we were separated from those who were carrying the body by shots being fired between them and us, and we were hurried by the guard back into the Lines. Not even the father was permitted to follow the corpse which was taken possession of and buried by people outside the Lines.

While no organized attack was made during the whole of our twenty-two days inside the Police Lines we knew perfectly well that they could wipe us off the face of the earth at any moment if only they had the courage to boldly close in on us and make the attempt. This they did not do; but day after day there was firing into the Lines from the surrounding jungles, usually at too great a distance to do much harm. Finally we got a helio message that there was a Relief Column on the way up the Mountains and for us to keep up good courage. The telegraph line had been cut and miles of the wire pounded up into bullets to shoot us with. I ought not to say "us" for several of the leading chiefs sent me word that I need not fear, that I had always been their friend and they would not harm me. And I really believe that they would not have intentionally done so.

The weather was so foggy that it was seldom a helio message could be put through; besides, the helio station was constantly watched by snipers and men had to crawl on their stomachs all the way up the mountain at greatest risk to themselves, and watch their chances to receive messages. But finally a message came telling us that the Relief Column would probably arrive the following day. This was a great comfort, for our provisions were exhausted, there only being short rations *for one day* when this message reached us! The Assistant Superintendent took all the sepoys he dared to withdraw from the station, leaving our Karen teachers and Chin Christians and a few sepoys in the trenches and started out to clear the way for the Relief Column. They had to fight their way through obstructions and snipers and were thirteen hours making twelve miles. One of their men was killed and three wounded when they met the Relief Column which had sustained a similar number of casualties. Major Burne, in charge of this column, made an unprecedented march, traveling day and night, without food, through difficult and dangerous mountain passes, and for some distance fighting his way to get there. For this splendid and heroic service he was decorated by his Government. When we saw 350 well-armed and -trained sepoys, accompanied by five British officers, including our Superintendent, come marching into Haka—Well, "it looked good" to us! They brought provisions and we had a hilarious evening. During the next few days they were busy clearing the surrounding country and opening the roads which had been strongly barricaded. They had some thirty or forty casualties and one British captain got a bullet in his arm. What those days meant to me, the only white woman in all that excited mob, is beyond description. I spent the time going among the wives of the sepoys and the sick and wounded men trying to cheer them up and give what courage and comfort I could. Several wounded sepoys died in the room next to us.

 The Superintendent told me that as soon as the roads were cleared I must leave the Hills until things were in a more settled condition. I protested, saying that my people had never needed me so much as at that time, that I was not afraid and that I would feel like a deserter to leave them. But it was no use. He was obdurate. He said he had not a sufficient force to protect me and at the same time settle the surrounding country; that if anything happened to me he would be responsible to the Government of both my country and his and that he asked *as a personal favor* that I go without further protest. There was nothing else to do. Accordingly a few days later in the company of the captain with a bullet in his arm, who was going to a place where he could have it located and removed, and with a mounted guard of thirty armed men I rode out of Haka with no idea of when I would be allowed to return. We had only traveled about seven miles when, turning a bend in the road, we ran onto a company of about thirty men evidently trying to make their way to the main army. They were armed with knives, bows and arrows, spears and one or two guns. Our guard surrounded them and they begged for mercy. Neither captain nor sepoys could speak their language so I had to act as interpreter while they were being disarmed and sent by a small but well-armed guard to Haka.

When we reached the camp at the end of the first march we found the bungalow in ashes where the Chinese caretaker had been killed. We rode on six miles further and camped by the Pao River. It was bitterly cold and we had to sleep on the ground, which was very stony.

I traveled in company with Captain Adams for five days. We were then past the danger zone and I went on alone with one Chin Christian and one mounted sepoy guard. Nine days later I reached Rangoon in safety—a little weary to be sure, but still "going strong." I remained in Lower Burma for three months and while there put a new Hymn Book and my translation of the Acts of the Apostles through the Press. Up to this time we had only a small Hymn Book of forty-two hymns translated by Mr. Carson, but during the Woodins' regime Mrs. Woodin, a sweet singer, had roughly translated a large number which she had not been able to finish and put in condition for printing before she left. These I carefully went over and typed for printing and added sixteen of my own translation. We had sung the hymns in the old book so many times that it was a great joy to the Christians to have a new book of more than one hundred and twenty-five hymns.

My sojourn in the plains also gave me an opportunity to visit Miss Whitehead in Maulmain and see something of the splendid work carried on there by our Mission—the Morton Lane Girls' School, the English-speaking Girls' School, the great Pwo Karen School, the Burmese Boys' School, the Tamil and Telugu School, the Orphanage and the beautiful Ellen Mitchell Hospital. My heart swelled with pride and thanksgiving to God when I saw the fine buildings and the hundreds of earnest, interested students all of whom were coming daily under beautiful Christian influences. What a mighty power toward the uplift of the nation—our Mission Plant in that one city! Then I had also an opportunity to revisit Bassein, the scene of my first Missionary endeavor and contrast present conditions with those of more than thirty years before. It was wonderful! I attended the Associational meetings where the delegates numbered into thousands—clean, cultured, well-dressed Christian people met to discuss and plan for the things of the Kingdom of God! The order, the intelligence, the beautiful music, the generous giving! Oh, it was wonderful, wonderful! And how my heart was touched when Yaba, who had been educated at Colgate and was a teacher when I was in Bassein thirty years before, now an old man, came to the platform and said he wanted to sing once more for "Mamma Hardin" (Carson). His sweet sympathetic tenor voice was clear as a bird's and brought the tears to my eyes. Again my heart was melted when a successful pastor came and with a husky voice and warm handclasp said that but for the help I had given him, many years before, he would never have been able to carry on the Lord's work. Hardships in Mission Work? Yes, but oh, the compensations!

Mr. Cope was not required to leave the Hills and he held things together better than I had dared to hope was possible. I left in December and returned in March. I superintended the school, did some teaching, translated the Sunday School lessons but devoted myself mainly to the revision of the gospels and the preparation of a dictionary.

CHAPTER 28

DEALING WITH FAMINE AND "FLU"

While trying to gather up the broken threads we suddenly realized that a famine was imminent. In settling the country after the insurrection, several villages had been burned with large quantities of food. The villages that turned against the Government at the time of its greatest need had to be punished. They were put at making roads and making an artificial lake. When they should have been in their fields they were making ammunition or later doing this forced labor. The result was a terrible shortage of food. For a time there seemed to be no food anywhere at any price. One of the leading chiefs told me that for two months he had not had any food whatever except "banhtaw" which is the boiled sprouts of the banana tree. He said there were thousands in the same condition. We feared for our Christians. There was simply no food and no money to buy it with. While shut up in the "Police Lines" I had written a letter to the Calvary church, Pasadena, which was interested in our work. I had not asked for money, but in their great-hearted way, in order to show their sympathy and have a part in the work, a lady sent me fifty dollars to use at my own discretion. The Church and Sunday School added to it. It reached me at the time of our greatest need. I still had the money given to me by members of the First Church, Pasadena, "for comforts on the voyage." I had put it in the P. O. Savings Bank as an emergency fund. With this and what other money I could scrape together I sent men down to the plains to buy rice. People were so weakened from insufficient food that I found it difficult to find men able to go so far and carry loads back; but finally we got them started, one hundred and fifty strong, as I remember it, and one man to do the buying and superintending. They traveled down the mountains for three days, spent one day resting and buying, then each with a gunny bag of seventy pounds of rice on his back, they made their way back up the steep mountains—making the trip, loaded, in five days. There was great excitement when they arrived; people crowding around, hollow-cheeked and hungry-eyed, in the hopes of getting something. I parceled out the rice, giving first to the sick and to those who had little children. I gave to widows and orphans, but made those pay who could afford to do so. When the men had rested and had a few nourishing meals I sent them back for more; and so the hunger was arrested among our Christians.

When news began coming in from the jungle villages of deaths from starvation, the Government made every effort to get food up the mountains as quickly as possible and made loans of money to the people with which to buy it. But the influenza came before people had regained their normal strength.

Mr. Cope started down the mountains to meet his wife and baby boy on their way out from America. When he reached Falam he learned that the influenza had broken out among the sepoys. He was asked to remain a few days. Every precaution was taken, but they felt that some of the few British there might be taken at any moment and that it would be terrible not to have some one there who could give a Christian burial. While waiting in Falam several cases appeared among the sepoys in Haka. I was there alone and Mr. Cope, upon hearing of it, immediately returned. The first one to die in Haka was the only source of medical help—an Indian Babu in charge of the Government Dispensary. He was very ill and the natives were afraid to go near him. Mr. Cope went again and again with food, medicine and disinfectants but not being able to give him sufficient care when so far away, he brought him down to the Mission Hospital. Every care was given him, but he soon passed away. By this time the disease had reached the Chins. In their weakened condition they had no power of resistance and many died, including Haka's biggest chief. Mr. Cope and I both went among the people doing what we could to relieve their suffering, taking them milk, soup, tea and medicines and ministering to them in every way we could. Finally, after three weeks of this, the crest of the wave seemed past and Mr. Cope started the second time to Rangoon to meet his wife and baby. He had not been gone long when cold rains set in and the wave returned with increased strength and swept away hundreds of victims. It was terrible. There were as high as ten deaths a day in our village. No one was coffined—though that was not unusual—but there were not well people enough to decently bury the dead. I kept my cook busy making broth, soup and tea, and I went daily from one hut to another taking things to them and caring for them as best I could. In many houses I would find people lying about on the floor—they have no beds—in various stages of the disease, sick, dead and dying, and not one able to so much as give a drink of water to the others.

There was one pathetic picture that will always remain with me. The Prospect Avenue Church of Buffalo, New York, had sent us a Christmas box. Besides the many other beautiful and useful things sent, there were some little, bright toy parasols about the size of a dinner plate. I do not suppose any gift of any price ever carried greater joy to the hearts of those who received them than those little parasols carried to the hearts of my little brown girls.

I went into a house where I heard there was sickness and found the father, mother, and three children lying on the floor too ill to raise their heads, and a little five-year-old girl sitting on the ground just outside holding on her knees her dying baby brother over whose head she was holding her most precious treasure—her little bright parasol.

Notwithstanding the many people who died and the fact that there were thirteen houses in Haka left empty by the ravages of influenza, *there was not one Haka Christian who died during this epidemic.* This made a profound impression on Christians and non-Christians alike. The fact that during the famine, thanks to Pasadena Christians, though no family had sufficient food all Christians had some that was nourishing and that having taken the hogs from under their houses the sanitary conditions were better, and that they had superior care during their sickness, added to the fact that God answers prayer, explains to my mind how they so wonderfully escaped death when others were dying all about them.

When the second wave had passed and the people, wan and miserable, were beginning to get about again, I took the influenza myself.

I was alone—not another white person in the station at the time. I ran a high temperature for three days and all the people in the place were frightened and anxious. They crowded into my room by scores and the first question was always the same: "Boinu, do you think you will die?" "It will be hard if you die. We will not know what to do if you die." My cook, a man, would come with solemn face to the door every few moments and say "Boinu, shall I make you some tea or some 'shoop' [soup]?" I wanted nothing in the world but to be left alone. I could not keep the people from filling my room. This got so on my nerves that I was simply obliged to get up and be well. And this is what I did. I telegraphed the Copes that I had "flu" and that they had better delay bringing the baby until danger of taking it was over. But instead of delaying they made every effort to reach me at the earliest possible moment. Mrs. Cope again relieved me of the housekeeping and superintending the hospital, where, though we had no doctor, we had a daily clinic with the help of Tsan Dwe, a Chin Christian who had been carefully trained in first aid and simple remedies under Dr. Woodin. We worked hard that year and with almost unbelievable success, considering the disintegrating influences of the insurrection, the famine and the influenza which followed so closely upon the heels of one another.

The strain of all these things, and being alone so much of the time while they were going on, had told upon me and I was planning to come home when my furlough would be due the following year. But one day a little less than a year after her arrival a cable message came to Mrs. Cope that her mother was seriously ill and requested her to come home. Mrs. Cope was an only daughter and had promised her mother that if the time came when her coming was really necessary a cable message would bring her. She had left her little boy, the oldest one, with the mother, now so ill. She felt obliged to go at once—and did so. Her mother was gone when she arrived and conditions at home made it necessary for her to remain. Her husband has been—and still is—laboring on alone during the four years that have intervened.

CHAPTER 29

A GREAT OPPORTUNITY—
PROVIDENTIALLY MET

When Mrs. Cope left I felt that I must put my furlough a year or two ahead and confidently hoped to round out a full forty years of service. But it seemed that was not to be. After the insurrection and the difficulty in settling the country the Chin Hills were visited by the Commissioner—the highest British officer under the Lieutenant Governor. He called on me and said during his visit, "Mrs. Carson, I have a proposition to make to you. [I was in charge of the school work.] Our Government has been administering these Hills for thirty years and I find that only one of the many Haka chiefs can write his own name. This one was one of your school boys and, by-the-way, is one of the most promising chiefs we have. Now what I want to propose is this:— That we build a dormitory to accommodate twenty of the succeeding sons of the leading chiefs, with quarters for a teacher, we furnish food and a cook for them and put these boys into your school. Would you take them on those conditions, if we would furnish the salary of the extra teacher required?"

I replied that our work was primarily religious, that the chiefs objected to having their children become Christians and that I would not consent to anything that would hamper the teaching of Christianity in the school. "Oh, teach them all the Christianity you want to. I don't suppose it will hurt them any," he said. "Good," I replied, "but there is another consideration. In your Government schools you have Buddhist teachers. I would not put a Buddhist teacher in my Christian school." "Well, that is easily arranged," he said. "I will allow you to appoint the teacher yourself, and I will confirm whatever appointment you make provided only that the teacher is qualified for his job."

What more could I ask? Twenty of the succeeding sons of the leading chiefs in our Mission school under daily Bible instruction and constant Christian influence. What a wonderful opportunity for uplifting the race! But how came we to have a teacher with normal training, making it possible to fulfill the one condition insisted upon by the Commissioner? This is the story:

THE STORY OF RE LEIN,
THE WAIF WHO BECAME A TEACHER

One of the awful scourges of diseases that so often comes to oriental villages came to a large village not far from Falam, the Government headquarters of the Chin Hills. Many people died and in one family only one little boy about four years old was left. The Superintendent went to investigate conditions after the plague and was told of this little child with no one to care for him. They had just opened the first Government school in the Chin Hills at Falam at that time and the Superintendent said he would take the little boy and put him into the School (it was a boarding school) and that he would personally be responsible for his food and clothing. He did as he promised and all went well for a time. But after a few months the Superintendent went to England on leave and there was no one interested in the child. He was a bright, mischievous little fellow and no doubt annoyed the cruel Burman teacher. Anyhow one evening an Indian sepoy Havildar was riding from Falam to Haka. On the road several miles distant from any house he found a little bunch of humanity lying with face to the ground sobbing his heart out. He picked the little fellow up and asked where his home was. "I haven't any home," was the reply. "Then where are your father and mother?" asked the Havildar. "I haven't any father and mother," said the child, weeping afresh. "Well, where do you stay?" persisted the Havildar. "The Boipa put me in the school but the teacher beat me and I ran away and I'll never go back. Look at my back," he said, with flashing eyes. "I'll never, *never* go back." The Havildar found his back marked with red welts showing that he had been cruelly whipped. He took the little fellow up on the pony in front of him and brought him to Haka. Having no beds nor any place to lay a little baby down, it is always tied to somebody's back. The little boy Re Lien became the baby carrier for the wife of the Havildar. A few months later, however, the Havildar was transferred to the plains. As he could not take the poor little Chin orphan with him he brought him to me, told his story and asked if I would take him. I took him, clothed him, fitted up a little room at the end of my cook house for him and put him into school. He was a bright little chap and I became very fond of him. I did my writing and reading evenings. He would come in and stand on the opposite side of my writing desk and chatter like a magpie. One evening I said, "Re Lien, you *must* keep quiet. I have a report to write and you bother me." With a very grieved look he said, "Boinu, I thought you would be so lonesome here alone. That is why I came." I told him then that I liked to have him there but that there were times when I could not talk to him, at other times we would have some fine visits and I would tell him stories. He went home happy, but after that he would always ask, "May I talk to-night?" and it was good to see the little face brighten when I said, "Yes." He would ask me to tell him about Joseph or Moses or the Rich Man and Lazarus or the Ten Virgins. He was entranced with these stories in particular, and would often be heard telling them to the other children.

There were prizes offered in school to those who passed highest in their Bible examination. Re Lien took first prize for three succeeding years. He went on to school until he passed the highest standard we taught, then I sent him to Falam and had him board with the Karen Evangelist while he attended the Government School for a year. I then sent him to Mandalay, had him board at our Baptist Mission School and take training in the Government Normal School. He finished the course and got his certificate before he was old enough to teach (eighteen) according to the law. Then with financial help from dear friends in Los

Angeles I sent him to Rangoon to our Theological Seminary. He was very ill and spent long, weary weeks in the hospital and finally had to return to the Hills on account of his health before he finished the course. He had only reached Haka a short time before the Commissioner's visit. So there was the man the only northern Chin man in the world with Normal training, ready to fulfill the Commissioner's condition. I appointed him and the appointment was confirmed, the arrangements to be completed in time for the next school year.

CHAPTER 30

SEVERING TENDER TIES

Major Browne, the Battalion Commandant of the military forces in the Chin Hills, came to Haka with the Commissioner. He told me that I had been through so many hard things that I simply *must* get away from Haka for the vacation as soon as school closed. He asked me to come and spend the vacation in Falam with his wife, saying that if I did not come he would surely come and bring me. And that is what he actually did. Mr. Cope was touring among the villages and I was in the station alone. Major Browne came over bringing a pony for me to ride, pack mules to carry my kit and a man to care for them. There was nothing to do but to go, and go I did. The pleasant ride and delightful companionship, the beautiful home, the lovely flowers, the winsome little daughter and charming wife—how I reveled in it all! How good to be free, for a few days, from all responsibilities, away from sordid surroundings where it was not necessary to listen continually to tales of trouble and sorrow and suffering! How restful and delightful it all was! But it was too good to last. I had been there just a week when I became very ill. The wife of the Superintendent took me into her own home where there was more room and I could have better care. My own people could not have been kinder. Every possible comfort was provided and every conceivable loving service rendered. The doctor said when I was better and felt that I must return to Haka, that I must be carried on a stretcher and that as soon as the rains were over I must return to America with no thought of ever returning to the Chin Hills. This was heartbreaking. I had so hoped to finish out forty years of service and to complete the translation of the New Testament. I could not, however, fail to be thankful to God and to my good English friends that I was in Falam where I could have every care when this illness overtook me, instead of being in Haka alone with nobody to do a thing for me except my kind-hearted cook, who would urge me every few moments to let him make me some "shoop."

Mr. Cope felt very strongly that I ought not to remain a day after it was possible to get away lest I stay too long and not be able to get away at all. When it became known among the natives that I must go to America, leaving the Chin Hills probably never to return, people came in from all directions and began "to weep and to break my heart."

The day before I left, two Hindu men, who had no interest in Christianity, but whose little boys had been in our school, came to say good-by. One of them said I had been both father and mother to his children and he wanted to make me a little gift and thereupon presented me with five rupees. The other one, with tears in his eyes, actually kneeled down and kissed my feet.

The Christians and school children, all unknown to, me, collected money for a parting gift. They went to Mr. Cope and with his advice and help, notwithstanding unbelievable poverty, procured for me a gift that cost more than a hundred dollars—a beautiful leather dressing case with silver-mounted fittings. How these expressions of loving appreciation touched my heart it is impossible to put into words.

Oh, how hard it was to leave the poor people among whom I had lived and labored for so many years. How hard to leave Mr. Cope to carry on alone without a kindred soul in sympathy with the work so dear to him. How hard to leave the little red-roofed cottage on the hillside every nook and corner of which was filled with precious memories. And, oh, how unspeakably hard to look for the last time upon the little sacred spot under the pines—the last resting place of the one who had so gladly given his life for the people.

The last day came, and very early in the morning people began gathering to see me off, many of the women weeping and with their blankets over their heads indicative of mourning. When I rode up the hill at the back of my house, I found the chiefs gathered to say good-by. There were men among them who in earlier days had done all they dared to retard our work. It was one of these who stepped forward and said, "Boinu, this is a sad day for the Chins. We do not want you to leave us. You have been our mother for many years. When you are gone, we will be like orphans. We are very sad." "Yes," said another. "When the Boinu has gone, we will be just like a flock of little chickens when a jungle cat has caught the hen." Scores of people followed me for miles. I implored them to return, but it was only when it began to rain that they turned their tear-stained faces homeward.

The rain increased so that we were soaked to the skin before we reached the little bungalow where we were to camp for the night. But we had sent food and clothing on ahead and were soon dry and comfortable.

The next day we rode through thick fog and heavy mist all day. That night "the windows of heaven were opened . . . and the waters prevailed and were increased greatly upon the earth." It was still coming down in torrents when we mounted our ponies in the morning, and though I wore a raincoat every thread of my clothing was soaked before I had been a half hour in the saddle. I had loaned my umbrella to some schoolgirls who were traveling with us on their way home. We had been invited to put up at Major Browne's and remain over Sunday in Falam. When within four miles of that place we encountered a landslide.

The whole side of the mountain seemed to have slid down over the road and the heavy rain had softened it to thick mud. There was no way of getting around it and we stopped and deliberated for some time. Finally Mr. Cope said, "I will see if I can get through and if I succeed I will come back and lead your pony." With frightened floundering, the mud coming to his pony's body, he somehow struggled through. I called to him not to come back, that he would be submerged in the mud, and hastened to "enter the fray" before he had time to tie his horse and wade in. My pony went in a little too far down, sank in the soft mud to his sides, became frightened and began to rear and plunge. Mr. Cope called to me to "Roll off, roll off!" Glancing up to learn what he was saying, I rolled off without any effort on my part, and now it was my turn to flounder in the mud which seemed bottomless. When I pulled out one foot, the other sank deeper. With my hands I tried to find some spot where the earth was firm enough to hold my weight, but only succeeded in running my arms their full length in the mud.

Eventually as I crawled to ground upon which I could stand, Mr. Cope called out, "Are you hurt?" "No, I am not hurt," I replied with considerable acidity in my voice. He put his hands on his hips, threw his head back and laughed till the tears came, saying as he did so, "My kingdom for a kodak! My kingdom for a kodak! You look just like a water buffalo!"

After this mud bath without any opportunity to wash or even scrape the mud from my plastered garments, I was obliged to mount and ride in that shocking condition into Falam. We had only ridden a short distance when we came to a second landslide. This time we dismounted and waded. As there were occasional stones to step on and saplings to grasp, although the sharp stones in the mud bruised and cut us, we got through with less difficulty. Can you imagine the picture of the two missionaries as they rode into the beautiful grounds of the home of the Commandant?

Fortunately Mrs. Browne was a large woman. She soon had dry clothing of her own and a warm bath ready for me. Thirty men were sent out to help our men with the pack mules through the landslides before we could have dry clothing of our own.

We rested over Sunday in Falam. On Saturday night I was given a farewell dinner to which all the white people in the station, numbering six, were invited. Mr. Daun, whom I had entertained *on his own venison* when on the way up the Hills more than twenty years before, claimed the privilege of giving the dinner. He had known me longer than the others. It was a wonderful dinner for the Chin Hills and was both a happy and a sad occasion.

As I write these lines there comes to me a letter from Major Browne in which he calls me his "second mother."

On Sunday Mr. Cope conducted a religious service in Major Browne's drawing room at which all English-speaking people in the place were present.

The nine miles between Falam and the Manipur River is very steep and we walked all the way, walking down four miles in the evening to the village where we stayed for the night. Next morning when we started out it was pouring rain; but this time I had a raincoat and umbrella and hoped to avoid a soaking before riding into the high altitude on the other side of the river. When we had only traveled about two miles, however, we met a bullock train of eighty pack animals on the narrow shelf of a mountain. Although I hugged the bank the packs struck me twice.

In trying to dodge a third one, I fell and smashed my umbrella into smithereens. Tossing it into the jungle I went on taking the downpour without protection and was soon soaked to the last thread of my clothing. Arriving at the river, we were obliged to mount in our soaked condition and ride for fourteen miles zigzagging all the way up higher and higher mountains until we reached the cold atmosphere of Lamban, where we had to wait for about four hours, without fire, before our dry clothing reached us. But we were near a Christian village and many of the people came to see us, bringing fruit, fowls, and vegetables and we had a nice though sad visit with them. Two Christian young men whom I had never seen before each slipped a rupee into my hand "to help buy food on the journey."

After this we traveled with good roads and little discomfort until the day we reached the plains. Leaving Fort White, at an altitude of about nine thousand feet, we rode down a gradual descent for six miles, then as the descent became steep for riding and hard on the ponies, we dismounted and walked the remaining ten miles to Camp No. 2. The road was very stony, and coming to lower and lower level, the heat increased until it became almost intolerable.

I knew that there was a Christian village to be passed some distance off the road and I tried to forestall having to go to it by saying, "Now, Herbert Cope, don't you dare suggest going out to the Christian village. I am perspiring at every pore, and my feet are frightfully blistered. I simply cannot stand it." "All right," he said, "but I am afraid the people will be badly disappointed." Miles before we reached where the jungle trail turned off to the village, in groups of twos and threes the Christians began to meet us.

When we reached the trail, I did not even suggest that I ever had any other thought than to go to the village. I would not have failed to do so for anything. When we got there, all of the people in the village except three or four who were sick, were congregated in their little zayat, or worship place awaiting us. We had a tender little farewell service with them, weeping and praying together. Then they began to bring me gifts of bananas, cucumbers, sweet potatoes, eggs and chickens. When one woman placed forty-two eggs at my feet, I said, "Oh, please don't bring so many things. You need these, and I don't. I know you love me. Just give me two chickens and a few eggs and take the other things back. We cannot carry them anyhow."

"Oh, Boinu, please take them all. We want to give you something and we haven't anything else to give," they said. "But we cannot possibly carry them all," I said. "Never mind. We will never see your face again and we all want to give you something. We will send somebody to carry them for you," they answered. And that is what they did. Practically the whole village followed us for a long distance, and we had difficulty in persuading them to return. "We will never see the Boinu's face again. Let us go a little farther," they said again and again.

The next day we reached the last bungalow before taking boats to go down the Myittha River, which would connect us with the outside world. Here we rested over Sunday, and here I wrote the last word in a Chin dictionary of over nine hundred pages. Though very imperfect and badly done, I trust and believe that it will be of value to those who come after me. May they be permitted to lead the people to far higher, holier ground than they have yet been able to attain.

Are there sacrifices and hardships in missions? Yes, many and very real ones. But what sacrifice can counter-balance the joy of giving to a people the Word of Life in their own language? Or the touching of darkened lives to uplift and ennoble? There are hardships and sacrifices in every strong, purposeful, worth-while life and there are equalizing compensations.

THE END

A MESSAGE FROM FOUNDATIONS OF GRACE PUBLISHING

We are so thankful for you, and we hope this book has been a blessing and an encouragement!

We'd love to hear from you if it has.

Would you be willing to leave us a review or sign up to be added to our mailing list?

If so, please go to FoundationsOfGracePub.org and enter your name and email address and a short, or long, note to us, letting us know who you are and how this book spoke to you. If you do, we'll send you something special.

We also print our books ourselves and sell them through our website.

In the coming years, we hope to offer dozens of brand new products on a variety of subjects from biography, theology, children's books, fiction, and more. We'll have hardbound, paperback, audio, and e-book versions of all of our materials as well. We hope to hear from you soon.

To give a gift to our ministry please go to MissionToMyanmar.com.

You can also register to receive our regular ministry updates about the ongoing work.

For the King and His Kingdom,

M. A. ROBINETTE

www.ingramcontent.com/pod-product-compliance
Lightning Source LLC
Chambersburg PA
CBHW051342040426
42453CB00007B/371